Asperger's Syndrome
and Jail

Asperger's Syndrome and Jail

A SURVIVAL GUIDE

Will Attwood

Jessica Kingsley *Publishers*
London and Philadelphia

First published in 2019
by Jessica Kingsley Publishers
73 Collier Street
London N1 9BE, UK
and
400 Market Street, Suite 400
Philadelphia, PA 19106, USA

www.jkp.com

Library of Congress Cataloging in Publication Data
A CIP catalog record for this book is available from the Library of Congress

British Library Cataloguing in Publication Data
A CIP catalogue record for this book is available from the British Library

ISBN 978 1 78592 371 5
eISBN 978 1 78450 713 8

Printed and bound in the United States

For Ben,

Your wisdom and support made all this possible.

Contents

Acknowledgements   *9*

Disclaimer   *11*

Introduction   *13*

Part 1 The Road to Jail   **17**

Ch 1   Pathways to Incarceration   19

Ch 2   The Watch House/Holding Cells   30

Ch 3   Different Types of Jails   47

Ch 4   Transport   57

Ch 5   The Big Question   62

Part 2 Practical Jail   **73**

Ch 6   So, You've Arrived   74

Ch 7   Medical   87

Ch 8   A Normal Day in Prison   102

Ch 9   Drugs in Jail   114

Ch 10   Keeping Busy   125

Ch 11   Jail Basics   147

Part 3 Social Navigation   **179**

Ch 12   General Social Advice   181

Ch 13   Sharing a Cell   194

Ch 14   Social Interaction with Other Inmates   204

Ch 15   Interacting with COs and Other Staff   230

Ch 16   Avoiding Confrontation   241

Ch 17   Coping Mechanisms   259

Ch 18   Pre-Jail, Post-Jail   279

         Glossary   *292*

         Index   *297*

Acknowledgements

This was not an easy book to write: deciding what was relevant to put in and what wasn't required a lot of reliving my time inside. While I have grown from my prison experience, and feel richer for having been through it, it would be a lie to insinuate that I wasn't scared, lonely and desperate at times.

Dredging up these previously tucked-away memories was difficult, but very, very necessary. This book holds no punches – it describes jail just the way it was. No embellishment, no down-playing.

The advice comes from my own experiences, observed interactions and conversations with inmates. These inmates were doing sentences for all manner of crimes, from public nuisance to serial murders. Their time behind bars ranged from 28 days all the way to life with little chance of being released.

In this regard, I would like to acknowledge all the men and women doing time, regardless of how long and where they are doing it. If not for them, there would be no need, and no source material, for this book.

If you're reading this in jail, or perhaps before sentencing, stay strong – I did, and I came out a stronger, wiser, more philosophical individual.

On a personal level, I must say a massive thank you to my Mum and Dad, who saw me through the dark times both in jail and out. This also applies to my sisters – I know you have always seen the potential in me, even when I couldn't.

I would also like to thank Matty H, Matty S, Hilly and Tracy for all having faith in me – you believed this book would come to fruition during times when I felt like giving up, and I can't tell you how much that helped. True friends are a rare and precious commodity.

On a final note, I must express my deep gratitude to Dawn and Annette for being there to listen when things felt like they were overwhelming me and, perhaps more importantly, for seeing me through the technical side of formatting the manuscript.

Disclaimer

This book is a guide only, designed to give basic advice regarding behavioural conduct while incarcerated. Because every human is unique, and every person with autism spectrum disorder (ASD) has their own manifestation of it, it would be literally impossible to write a comprehensive text that addresses all possible scenarios which may arise. Having said that, jails have more similarities than differences, so practical information such as how phone accounts work and how to organise visits will be largely applicable, regardless of jurisdiction. People too have more similarities than differences, so, while the set-up of a jail unit in Australia may vary from one in England, the inmates residing there will have a lot of similarities – most will be there on parole breaches, most will be there because of drug-related crime and most will be doing shorter sentences (one to six years). As such, the advice provided in this book is likely to be helpful for all inmates with ASD, irrespective of where they're doing time and for how long. Also, the book strongly recommends inmates with ASD use their diagnoses to be allocated to a suitable unit, where there is comparatively little violence. It doesn't matter what country you're in, an ASD-friendly unit is an ASD-friendly unit. On that note, a run-of-the-mill unit is a run-of-the-mill unit, and this book addresses issues that can arise in those environments, and how to minimise negative experiences.

Naturally, the names of people in the first-person stories throughout the book have been changed to protect their identities, and no specific jails are identified.

The phrase 'watch, listen and learn' is used frequently, and for good reason. Not only is it a very good policy to live by while in jail, it also means the advice in this book can be applied to a wide range of scenarios – because you will have the time to work out who's who and so forth, and then apply what this book has taught you accordingly. Whether you're in Melbourne, Manchester or Miami, the core elements of jail etiquette remain the same.

Introduction

I wrote this book after serving two years of a three-year sentence for robbery. I wrote it because, as an 'Aspie' (or one with Asperger's syndrome), I found jail to be a socially complex environment, with its own rules, vernacular and swift 'justice' for indiscretions.

The primary objective of this book is to keep the inmate with autism spectrum disorder (ASD) as safe as possible while they do their time. If it looks like you, or someone you care for, is headed for the Big House, this book is meant to soothe rather than alarm you. Because people's fears of jail are based on cultural references (fiction books, movies, TV shows and carefully edited documentaries) rather than extended dialogue from an actual former inmate, there are many misconceptions floating around. This text aims to explain it just as it is, or at least as it was for me. I started in maximum security, mainstream prison, and finished my sentence in maximum security, mainstream prison. But my ASD made it complicated (at least at first), so I want to share some of my experiences as well as explain how jail works, what to do and what not to do. I received my diagnosis of ASD during my sentence, and this allowed me to move to a more suitable, less intense unit. This book explains in detail how you can go about this process. Because my jail experience was divided into two parts – the first half in tough units, the second in the special needs unit (SNU) – I can offer the reader insight into surviving in a mainstream prison, and speak with conviction when I say doing your time in an ASD-friendly unit can be the difference between misery and contentment.

Part 1: The Road to Jail looks at how people come to find themselves in such an intense situation as jail in the first place (because you don't just wake up in there one day, fortunately), how to start out right from the get-go, what to look out for and what to expect.

Pragmatic aspects of life behind bars are discussed in Part 2: Practical Jail. This part illustrates how prisons run, day-to-day activities, how to keep busy, how visits are organised, how to get work – basic stuff that's helpful to know in advance. It will also start to paint a picture in your head of what to expect. For Aspies, forewarned is forearmed.

Part 3: Social Navigation explains how the social hierarchy of jail manifests, how to maximise your chances of 'flying under the radar' (from both fellow inmates and correctional officers), the best ways to deal with various social situations and how to conduct yourself if things take a turn for the worse. Part 3 is *not* the only section of the book that looks at how ASD can affect an inmate's time inside. Interwoven through the entire text are pieces of advice explaining how ASD can affect the issue being addressed.

I went into jail with *some* idea of how it runs, through other addicts who had done time. This book has more information about jail than I ever learnt from my drug associates, and even their limited anecdotes helped me inside. I hope that I can help you feel more confident about what may await you. I've included personal anecdotes for illustrative purposes – to help you get a 'feel' for jail life through first-person accounts.

The only other pertinent information to give at this juncture is this: everybody walks their own path through incarceration. Nobody can do it for you. There is no way a book can possibly address every potential scenario, so I've written a *guide* – an examination of jail through the eyes of an Aspie, to help other Aspies. There is one piece of advice that I will impart now, and it won't be the first time you hear it – look, listen, learn. Three simple words with so much power. Keeping a low profile, keeping to yourself, spending time alone – these are the qualities that suit the inmate with ASD. They're also the qualities that will keep you from putting your foot in your mouth, appearing to try too hard and befriending inmates who turn out to be detrimental to your mental health. Keep it as a mantra – look, listen, learn.

Part 1
The Road to Jail

If you were to believe what you see on TV, the jail experience would be this: you commit a crime; a few days later you appear in court; and a few hours later you're running away from some fat guy called Bubba who wants to have his way with you. Obviously, the real process is a bit more complex. First, regardless of whether you are granted bail or not, you will spend at least some time in detention, in the police station itself or a facility built to accommodate people prior to their initial court appearance. This will be your first experience with deprivation of liberty – the very essence of incarceration. Because of the unusual and sometimes confronting nature of this experience, especially for somebody with autism spectrum disorder (ASD), a chapter is devoted to elaborating on what to expect in these early days, and how you should conduct yourself to minimise negative fallout, both internally and socially.

Another chapter is devoted to examining the different *types* of correctional facilities you may find yourself in during different stages of your incarceration. Again, it is not as simple as people might think – jails are not all the same, even in the same state/jurisdiction. Jails are subtly different, and have different, unspoken 'codes of conduct' – the nuances of which are important for someone with ASD to understand.

Transportation between these facilities is also addressed, because it involves very close proximity to other inmates, and long journeys can lead to long conversations, and the longer the conversation, the higher the risk you might say something you regret.

Finally, and perhaps most importantly, Part 1 of this book includes a chapter questioning whether to use your diagnosis in an official capacity, by letting the powers-that-be know you are on the spectrum, or whether to keep it to yourself. There are valid arguments for both positions. You may not *want* to be housed in a 'special' unit. It's arrogant to assume everyone with ASD will want that. And if you tell the authorities, there's a chance you may not have a choice – they may want to cover themselves legally and not risk putting you in run-of-the-mill units – essentially making the decision for you.

CHAPTER 1

Pathways to Incarceration

I was on edge already. My life wasn't exactly smooth sailing and my girlfriend had been even more difficult than usual. Then came the phone call. It was an associate. There are few friends in the drug scene, so associate is about as intimate as it gets.

The associate was accusing me of stealing his wallet. He was adamant I had taken it from his car earlier that day. I tried pointing out the logistical problems with his theory, such as the fact I hadn't been in his car that day, or any other day for that matter. And that I didn't need to steal because my habit was by and large taken care of through the methadone program. And that he associated with many, many unsavoury types, any of whom could have stolen his wallet. None of it mattered. None of it mattered. He wasn't listening. He'd been up for days and had long since stopped thinking in a logical manner. No matter what approach I used, he was convinced: I had stolen his wallet.

Ordinarily, this wouldn't have been too much of an issue. The problem was he knew about two armed robberies I had

*committed a month prior. I had been high, and needed to pay
a debt. He told me he wanted $800 or 'the cops will be around
your place by tomorrow evening'. The line went dead.*

*I slept restlessly that night. At one point, I dreamt about a
machine making great big thudding noises. As the fog of sleep
cleared, I realised the noise was real, and it was coming from
my front door. It was a cop-knock: loud, aggressive and very
assured. My associate had made good on his threat.*

*A week later I was in a unit built for 52 men but housing 80,
living with people who had done everything from breaching a
domestic violence order (DVO) to committing multiple murders,
and everything in between.*

A Lonely Journey

For most people, the idea of facing time behind bars is no more
than theoretical. If they have thought about it, it will have been
fleeting – a quick question like, 'I wonder how *I* would cope
locked up?' There are others who may have thought about it
more deeply, such as the relatives (or friends) of people who:

1. are facing possible (or probable) jail time
2. are currently incarcerated or
3. have been locked up but are now back in society.

Even then, these relatives/friends have the luxury of experiencing
jail by proxy and, while it may open their eyes and help them
understand, it's not the same as being there.

For people with ASD, the prospect of facing time behind bars
can be very scary. This is because their knowledge of jail is usually
based on inaccurate cultural representations (as mentioned
in the Introduction) and/or third- or fourth-hand stories that

have been greatly embellished. There are many misconceptions about how the police operate, how the judicial system operates and how prisons operate. This chapter (in fact this whole book) is written as a guide for people with very little or no experience regarding how the criminal justice system works. Specifically, it is written for people with ASD and those who love and care for them. Because you don't just get thrown in jail suddenly, for no reason, it's important to address *how* someone finds themselves behind bars.

Please note

- This book is not written by a lawyer – keep that in mind when any legal matters are discussed.
- Judicial procedure varies from state to state and country to country – this *is a guide only*.
- While you may have read or heard of a similar case to yours (or the person you are supporting), *do not* assume the process will be the same for you or your loved one. All cases are different, and will vary in terms of the severity of the offence, the impact on the victim(s), your criminal history (or lack thereof), your age and mitigating circumstances. No two cases are identical.
- This book is written to help people with ASD cope with jail; it is not written to help them beat the charge – that's the lawyer's job.

First things first: there are multiple ways one may come to be in a room with police officers, facing a possible charge. This chapter will examine the most likely sequence of events that will lead to such a scenario.

Police Raids

Having your personal, safe space invaded by hyped-up police officers is a negative experience for anybody. For those with ASD, police raids can be a particularly confronting experience. You can expect it to be:

- *A surprise* – Police use the element of surprise when executing a search warrant, so they often conduct raids in the early hours of the morning. People with ASD thrive on routine and familiarity – a police raid will automatically cause distress for someone with ASD because it upsets established protocol.
- *Noisy* – The police will have elevated adrenaline levels, even if the raid is on a 'benign' subject (an individual with no criminal history or no history of violence). They will be 'hyped up' and assertive, which means they will be loud. Being loud also means *everybody* in the dwelling knows what is happening, which helps the police maintain control. If you are sensitive to loud noises, try to remain calm – agitation *won't* help your situation.
- *Invasive* – Police raids, by their very nature, are invasive. Within seconds the dwelling is filled with multiple police officers. Usually they tell everybody to come to one room (usually the lounge room) and sit down. At this point the search will begin. For those on the spectrum, be prepared to have your personal effects rifled through. If you have a specific way you like to keep things in order, accept the police may put it *out* of order. Accept it. You can always rearrange later. Also, they may look through the belongings of others living in the dwelling, so be prepared to apologise to your housemates/family members if necessary.

- *Embarrassing* – Intrusion into your space by people (even police officers) can be embarrassing, especially if you're the target of the investigation. Police generally grant you the courtesy of explaining the charges (or nature of the investigation) to you in private – but not always. If the crime is of a particularly embarrassing or demeaning nature, such as a sex offence, it may be *deliberately* aired out loud – so if you're on the spectrum, be prepared for this. Police will sometimes try to humiliate you.

A police raid doesn't mean an arrest is imminent. They may not find what they're looking for, or if they're taking things away (like hard drives, phones or other types of evidence), these will have to be forensically examined before they can become evidence. However, for the purposes of this chapter, let's assume your next step is being placed under arrest.

Being 'Detained for the Purposes of Questioning'

Those with ASD will find being detained confronting – because your interaction with the police goes from theoretical to very real. An hour ago you were fast asleep. Now you're in handcuffs. This does not mean you are under arrest per se, but rather 'detained for the purposes of questioning'. Don't bother trying to run. Police have Tasers, cars and possibly dogs. Also, it doesn't look good in the eyes of the law if you try to abscond at the first opportunity.

Expecting to be cuffed is important, as people on the spectrum can be hypersensitive to tactile sensations. Handcuffs are *tight*, they may affect your *balance* and your general movement may be *restricted*. Don't worry too much about this – they will be removed after one of two things occurs:

- They find nothing incriminating, and must let you go.
- They find something incriminating, or they want to question you further. In this case, the cuffs will be removed once you are inside the local police station.

Being Interviewed

Please note

There are many variables regarding police raids, collection of evidence, detaining for questioning, actual arrests, the pressing of charges and so on. To cover them all would be time-consuming and ultimately pointless – this book is about coping with jail, not exploring every avenue people take to get there. This chapter is included because it's pertinent to illustrate how one might come to be behind bars, and the role your ASD could play in this process.

Even though you have been 'detained for the purposes of questioning', you *do not* have to answer any questions. You can ask for a legal representative (a lawyer) to be present, along with a support person (such as a parent, spouse or friend). A support person is potentially very helpful, especially if you find the whole concept of police and interviews intimidating. Your ASD could make you feel intimidated, especially if the police are being either overtly or passively aggressive. Having a support person there will significantly help reduce anxiety.

Practical issues
For people with ASD, there are a few practical things to mention about police interviews:

- Bright lights, often fluorescent, are common in interview rooms.
- The chairs may not be particularly comfortable.
- The temperature might be too hot or cold.
- The demeanour of officers/detectives may be abrasive and/or rude.
- Intimidation techniques may be used by detectives if they don't think you are cooperating.
- There may be proximity issues – detectives might try to 'get in your face' to disconcert and intimidate you.

Handling an interview

The attitude you adopt when conversing with the police is important. How you conduct yourself should be based on your individual circumstances:

- Are you truly innocent?
- Have you committed the crime but feel confident the police can't prove it?
- Are you guilty and intend to plead as such?

THE INNOCENT

If you are genuinely, 100 per cent innocent of the charges you are facing, it's a no-brainer that you should plead not guilty. Fortunately, miscarriages of justice are relatively rare, though this assertion could be challenged by minority groups or those residing in developing countries. If you find yourself in this situation:

- Explain yourself – if you have nothing to *hide*, then there's nothing to *find*.
- If the police are persistent, ask for a lawyer and say *nothing more* until the lawyer is present.

25

- Hopefully they will realise, sooner rather than later, that they are barking up the wrong tree.
- If, however, they *do* press charges, apply for bail at the first opportunity. Applying for bail will be explained to you by your legal representative.

PLAUSIBLE DENIABILITY

If you *are* guilty of the crime the police are trying to charge you with, but you think they have got very little evidence and are almost certainly relying on a confession – *keep your mouth shut*. Silence is your right; although you may think it makes you look guilty, that's irrelevant – the police can't charge you with failing to talk during an interview. Alternatively, wait until a lawyer is present before giving your version of events. Talking or remaining silent could well be the difference between jail and freedom. From an anecdotal perspective, it seems that a lot of inmates talk their way into jail, one way or the other, either slipping up with the police or telling associates, who then use this information against you to get themselves out of trouble – the dog, the rat, the snitch, the grass. Keeping your mouth shut is one of the best policies when it comes to the serious issues in life, and for people with ASD, this adage is even more relevant.

THE SMOKING GUN

Sometimes the police will have evidence that is nearly impossible to refute. Trying to explain away that evidence would be difficult at best, and downright impossible at worst. Ask yourself:

- Do I have a solid alibi?
- Has someone 'dogged' (told) on you?
- What do the police know that you don't?

- Are there records/documents pertaining to your guilt?
- Do you have prior convictions of a similar nature?
- Are you prepared to go toe-to-toe with an experienced interrogator?
- Will your ASD make lying difficult?

How you answer these questions will enable you to decide if it's worth fighting the charges. *Remember* – cooperation with the police, admitting your guilt and showing remorse from day dot will go a long way towards ensuring the best possible outcome for you in court. Inside, inmates don't hold it against other inmates who pleaded guilty to their charges – many people have good reason to. It's okay to say you admitted your guilt to the police, and will obviously plead guilty at court, which will be some months away. Don't, however, talk about how 'cooperative' you are with the police when behind bars. Inmates understand people do this to reduce their sentence, so it's okay, but it doesn't need to be mentioned. You can be honest if asked; just don't volunteer the information. Putting your hand up for your crime could be the difference between a *custodial* (i.e. you go to jail) or a *non-custodial* sentence (i.e. you are found guilty, but do not go to jail). You may instead be sentenced to:

- A term of imprisonment, *wholly suspended* – this means no jail *but* if you get so much as a possession charge during the designated time period, you will be sent to jail.
- An intensive correction order (ICO) – this means you will have to see a psychologist and complete certain courses to help you avoid reoffending.
- Community service – you will be ordered to perform a certain number of hours doing work for the community.

The Worst-Case Scenario

For serious crimes, to which you have admitted guilt to the police, or the police have sufficient evidence to charge you, you will be *remanded in custody*. This means you won't be going home, at least not for a while. This information can be difficult for the individual with ASD to grasp. Try to take it one minute at a time, then one hour at a time, then one day at a time. There have been other people with ASD in your situation, and they made it through – *so will you!*

If you are remanded in custody, a court-appointed solicitor will see you relatively quickly (weekends may slow this process), and you can organise to apply for bail at the next available opportunity. However, if the severity of your crime is high, and there is significant evidence against you, and you are considered a 'flight risk' (fleeing) and/or a danger to the community, bail is unlikely to be granted.

You will be kept in the watch house until the next transport is available to take you to a *remand jail*, where you will await trial or sentencing. Different types of correctional facilities will be discussed in Chapter 3.

> **Please note**
> Remember – any time spent locked up will count towards your total sentence. For example, if you get arrested for car theft on 1 January 2020, and stay locked up, on remand, for six months before sentencing in June 2020, that six months will count. So, if you get a nine-month sentence, you will have only three months left to go.

When the cops raided my tiny, dirty little unit, I was relatively certain I wasn't going to beat the charges. My scumbag associate had given me up, and I had no alibi. Besides, my life was a mess. I also wasn't prepared to try to get my girlfriend to concoct a false alibi – I knew that was asking too much of her. What tipped me over the edge was tripping, literally, over some drug paraphernalia on the floor. I stumbled and had to be steadied by one of the police officers. I knew it had to end there. I've never had what people describe as an 'epiphany', but this was close enough. I asked for one of my cigarettes, and the lead detective seemed reluctant. Bossy. In control. 'Why should I give you one of those?' he asked, his tone neutral. 'We're in the middle of a raid.' He looked slowly around my shabby apartment, his eyes eventually coming to rest on me. 'So,' he repeated, 'why would I give you a smoke?'

'Because if you do', I replied, 'I'll tell you about the two armed robberies I committed earlier this month, which is why I assume you're here.'

For the record, that was why they were there – I had seen it on the cop's paperwork, on the warrant.

He gave me my cigarette, and as I inhaled, and the nicotine took effect, I knew I had made the right choice. My life was a sad joke; a chaotic, drug-fuelled parody of normalcy, made worse by all the pretences I had been desperately trying to tell myself; a vain attempt to block out the harsh reality of broken dreams and failed opportunities. It was time for a change, and I knew it.

CHAPTER 2

The Watch House/ Holding Cells

> **Please note**
> Throughout this book the terms 'watch house' and 'holding cells' are, for all intents and purposes, interchangeable. For the sake of simplicity, from here on these facilities will be referred to as the 'watch house'.

Introduction

The watch house cells are the first place you will find yourself once you've been arrested and charged with an offence serious enough to justify holding you. These facilities are often underneath (or at least close to) either a police station or a courthouse. Relevant for the inmate with ASD, they hold only a *small number of inmates* and they hold them for a comparatively *short amount of time*.

It's important to emphasise that the watch house/holding cells are almost always staffed by police officers, *not* correctional officers (COs). What is the difference? Officers staffing the watch house are fully qualified members of the police force. Remember this – assaulting a police officer is a serious offence. Assaulting

THE WATCH HOUSE/HOLDING CELLS

a CO is also an offence, but is not considered by the courts to be as severe as bashing a cop. If your ASD makes you liable to be verbally abusive (or physically intimidating) when you are stressed, do your best to just hold it in. It's not worth it. Don't think for a second the police officers will tolerate nonsense. Plus, you don't want to transfer to jail with a mark against your name – that's a bad start.

Mainstream vs Protection

It is important to talk about the difference between 'mainstream' and 'protection'. Prisons generally work in a two-tier fashion – that is, they house both 'streams' of prisoner: protection and mainstream. *Most inmates are mainstream.* This is because most prisoners are incarcerated for drug-related crime.

Why do people go into protection?
Sometimes, an inmate won't have a choice but to be placed in protection. People who are charged with sex offences against children usually have no say in the matter. If you have been charged with a sex offence against a child, and for some bizarre reason you *are* offered mainstream, *don't go.* It is not an exaggeration to say that your life could be in danger. There's a reason protection exists – it's so people can leave jail on their own two feet, not in the back of an ambulance.
There are other reasons people go into protection, such as:

- People charged/convicted of sex offences against adult women but who are not naturally tough – there are some rapists of adult women (and men) who get by in mainstream, but they must 'prove' themselves to be dangerous; otherwise they *will* be relegated to protection.

- Police informants – people on the police payroll who have committed a crime that the police simply can't turn a blind eye to, and someone in mainstream knows their secret.
- Jailhouse informants – inmates who, for some reason, decided it would be a good idea to tell on other inmates, and got caught out.
- High-profilers – people who aren't criminals by nature, but have been charged with a serious crime (usually murder), and it has generated a whirlwind of publicity. They are at risk because some inmate will try to make a name for himself by assaulting 'that guy on the news'.
- Celebrities – some celebrities fare okay in mainstream (usually sporting idols), but your run-of-the-mill soap star who killed someone drink-driving will be run out of mainstream, mostly because prisoners are bored and may earn some status as being the guy who made the celebrity flee to protection.
- People who are in jail for a crime, but are testifying against someone else who played a more significant role in that crime. For example, a low-level drug dealer agrees to testify against his supplier in exchange for a reduced sentence. This is seen as a 'weak' choice by the prison population, so for his safety he needs to be in protection.
- People who have run up significant debt, either inside or on the outside, usually from drugs or gambling, and are unable to pay and have nowhere left to run.
- People who were bullied in mainstream to the point the prison authorities decided to move them for their own safety.
- People who *want* to move, because they feel threatened and have made several requests to move.

Prisoner movement is closely controlled, so mainstream inmates don't bump into protection inmates on the walkways. Placement jails are usually either *all mainstream* or *all protection*, for ease of prisoner movement and management. However, remand and reception jails usually have a two-tier policy. For more information about different types of jails, see Chapter 3.

When protection isn't a choice

The only time you *need* to go in protection is if you have committed a crime against a child (any sort of crime) or committed an underage sexual offence by proxy (downloading and/or distributing underage material). If your crime isn't of that nature, go for mainstream – you don't need to *start* jail where everyday criminals (armed robbers, drug traffickers, car thieves) would only come as a last resort. You should start in mainstream and, if things go pear-shaped, you have the option of protection as back-up. *It does not work the other way around!* People have tried to go from protection to mainstream in the past, and, from an anecdotal perspective, it simply doesn't work.

If you have been designated for protection, or made a choice to be in protection, your stay in the watch house will be no different from mainstream inmates, with the following exceptions:

- You will be processed separately from the mainstream inmates.
- You will be placed in a 'pod' or 'cell' either by yourself or with other protection inmates.

Don't lie. People have sometimes committed a crime considered morally abhorrent to inmates (such as hurting a vulnerable individual – a woman, a child, an elderly or disabled person), then figured they can 'make up a story' and it will all be okay. There's just one problem with this – you could come unstuck, and then you are in real trouble.

How might you come unstuck?

- Somebody who knows the truth (like a relative of the victim) ends up in jail too.
- Relatives/friends of the victim send correspondence pertaining to you and your true crime. This could also be done over the phone.
- You rub a CO up the wrong way and suddenly people start asking pointed questions.
- The inmates simply work on you enough (verbally), until a brick comes loose on your house of lies, and down it comes.

Those are just four of many possible ways for you to come undone. Bottom line: if you have committed a morally heinous crime, *never* try to lie your way through mainstream – it could get you seriously injured or worse.

> *I was never in protection, so I can only speculate about what life is like in there. My guess would be it's largely the same. There would be bullies, there'd be drugs, there'd be people who just minded their own business. I also suspect the same 'rules' regarding behaviour would apply. There would be plenty of tough inmates in protection; there would have to be. After all, it's jail. I would like to think the social advice (and the practical information) would be relevant for inmates with ASD across all forms of incarceration.*

The 'Prepped' Aspie

This book is written for people with ASD and, as those who have the condition (and their families) know, new environments are more intimidating for them than the average person, and jail by its very nature is intimidating. But don't leap to the conclusion that you won't be able to handle mainstream just because you have ASD. You also have pride, intelligence and, if need be, fists. Take, for example, the many people with ASD who reach out to substances to try to calm the racing, loud thoughts and irritating stimuli that follow us around like our shadows. If you're an addict with ASD, prison may not be too difficult. Why?

By the time an addict reaches the point where they are engaging in serious criminal acts to fund their habit, they have spent months or years associating with people who know the streets, understand the subtle codes of conduct (both with each other and authority figures), can decipher criminal vernacular and engage in criminal acts as a means to an end. These people have a massive head start over someone who has committed a white-collar crime, and has no understanding of the criminal world. People with ASD who have committed a drug-related crime, or those who aren't addicts but come from a crime family, or perhaps grew up in rough domestic conditions, usually fare quite well in jail. *Having ASD doesn't automatically mean jail will be extra difficult.* That's a simplistic way of viewing the issue.

Processing

The officers who process you are professional and adhere to the unspoken code of 'treat me with respect, and I'll extend you the same courtesy'. Communication between you and the officers should *always* be kept to a polite minimum; if, for example, your ASD makes you quite open about yourself, you should try to rein this in. Other prisoners are more likely to trust an inmate who is wary of authority (or at least appears to be).

If you are planning to defend against your charges, be particularly careful what you say, because:

- The people staffing the watch house are police officers.
- Everything that's said is potentially being recorded, including informal exchanges between you and officers plus you and other inmates.

Body Search

Upon arrival in the watch house, you will be taken to a private area by an officer of the same sex to do a brief search for contraband (drugs, phones, weapons, letters, etc.). This search is not overly invasive, but if your ASD means you have an aversion to being naked, or being near others *while* naked, remember this procedure is protocol and *be ready for it*. For someone with ASD, it is important to minimise unpleasant surprises. Body searches will become a relatively regular procedure during your time behind bars, and it gets a little easier each time.

The officer (or guard, as will be the case once you leave the watch house and move to the remand prison) will ask you to take off whatever you are wearing on your upper body. They will look through it, and, once they have deemed it safe, place it into a marked bag (Property of Prisoner X). You will then be given some clean prison clothes to dress your top half.

The officer will then request that you remove the bottom half of your clothes, including your underwear, which you place in a laundry bin. You will get these clothes back (washed) upon your release from incarceration.

A visual search of the lower half of your body is now conducted. The officer will not make physical contact with you. However, for men the procedure does involve you lifting your testicles. The officer then asks to look inside your mouth (a brief look, not a forensic dental analysis), and requests that you run your fingers behind your ears. If you have longer hair, they will ask you to run your hands through it thoroughly. They will also ask to see the bottom of your feet. *Cavity searches in most jurisdictions are illegal, and this includes the watch house. You are protected by the law. However, at the time of writing, some jails still ask inmates to 'spread their cheeks', so they can see if you have contraband resting between your buttocks.*

It is important to note that *at no point* will an officer make physical contact with you during your stay in the watch house. Of course, if you are violent and/or overtly provocative, they will use force if deemed necessary (remember – they *are* police officers).

Identifying Particulars

At some point, you will have your 'identifying particulars' taken. Identifying particulars are a routine procedure where photos (mugshots), DNA and fingerprints are taken, along with height and weight measurements. Any unique, permanent features such as tattoos, scars or birthmarks are documented. You will also be asked about medical and dietary requirements. *If you do have specific dietary requirements, whether they are medical, cultural or religious in nature, now is the time to let the authorities know.*

Your Phone Call

Everybody has heard the fabled 'Hey, cop, where's my phone call?' line in any given number of TV shows and movies, and it exists for a reason – you are indeed entitled to a phone call from the watch house. If the first number you try doesn't answer, you will most likely be able to try another number – just be *polite and patient*. Having said that, they *won't* let you sit on the phone, legs up on the table, dialling every number you can recall. If the number you need to reach isn't answering, they will let you try again in a few hours. Remember – keep calm.

If you have ASD, you may be feeling very anxious and in need of some form of contact with your 'pillar' – the most stabilising personal influence in your life. If you don't reach them on the first try, relax – the officers know people get stressed in this environment, and will endeavour to help you make contact – just don't hassle them. That's counterproductive. Also, *don't go and complain about it too much in front of the other inmates* – they're doing it tough too: like the young man whose girlfriend is eight months pregnant and he's stuck there, or the older bloke who's been picked up for drink-driving but needs to take his ailing mother to the specialist every Tuesday. You are legally entitled to your phone call, and the police know it. So, don't worry unnecessarily – you *will* get to contact the outside world.

Medical Needs

ASD and anxiety go hand in hand, so medication can be the difference between coping or becoming a very, very unhappy person. To increase the chance of getting your meds, use part of your phone call to ask somebody you know and trust (such as a parent, partner, sibling or primary caregiver) to bring the medication to the watch house. Obviously, the medications will need your name and details on them. The last thing they need is some medical mishap to occur, so for the most part you can expect compliance. Just stay calm!

If you can't reach someone helpful on the phone

A nurse will come around to see you within 24 hours of admission to the watch house. At this point you can tell them about your medicinal needs. The nurses are almost always compassionate and non-judgemental. If someone on the outside can't get your medication to you, the nurse will make sure you get it.

It may be worth memorising your prescribing doctor's number. Even if you can't remember it, don't stress. The nurse knows your name and will take care of you. They are very professional, and they will make sure you get your prescribed drugs. Again, stay calm!

A final note on medications

If you are worried about the jail taking you off medications you feel really help you cope with having ASD, like diazepam (Valium) or quetiapine (Seroquel), it is important to start the process of addressing this issue as early as possible. You will likely be in the watch house for at least a couple of days, and you will have ample opportunities to see the nurse. To see them ASAP, just tell the staff you really need someone to talk to because you are stressed (which is true) and you liked the nurse. The staff will usually comply, because the last thing they need is for someone to hurt themselves, only to have it come out *later* that the inmate asked for help. It's very important to get the ball rolling as early as possible regarding your medications because most things move slowly in jail.

Irrespective of whether you have told the authorities about your ASD diagnosis (see Chapter 5), you should always act politely and consistently, regardless of how wound up you feel, and how illogical the whole system can seem at times. Ideally, you want medical staff (both in the watch house and, later, in jail proper) to know you as polite and friendly, but also as someone who knows their rights and will persist until reasonable requests are met.

Life in the Watch House

Your stay in the watch house will be comparatively brief, probably not much longer than a week. It's physically uncomfortable and you may find yourself sharing a cell with people you don't like. This is rarely problematic. Even if other watch house inmates pick on you for being different, they're unlikely to expend much energy making your life difficult. This is because they too are suffering from the monotony and uncomfortable nature of their environment. They may also be detoxing from drugs, so may become introspective and lethargic.

ASD-Specific Issues

In terms of layout, all watch houses are quite similar. What they all have in common (from an anecdotal perspective) is the propensity to generate echoes, meaning *everything* seems louder. It will take some getting used to. If you have a significant problem with echoing, ambient white noise or the sound of the TV, you could ask the staff for some one-use-only ear plugs, after explaining your predicament. They should have them. People with ASD can be hypersensitive to unpleasant environmental stimuli, and unfortunately the watch house has a disproportionate amount of these. For example:

- fluorescent lighting
- loud and (sometimes) seemingly relentless conversations
- blaring television
- no fresh air, and possibly no natural light
- air conditioning kept low but constant
- no comfortable chairs or beds.

Remember – stay calm – your time here will be relatively short.

Behavioural Conduct

People with ASD, and those close to them, know all too well just how quickly things can degenerate during social situations. It can take time, professional intervention and a lot of support to develop the tools to handle challenging interactions. Therefore, it's important to remember that in a potentially aggressive environment such as the prison system, you must be as aware as possible of what you say. Sometimes it's better to say nothing and just watch, listen and learn.

Interacting

Despite the small size of the watch house, it is essential to follow 'prison protocol'. Part of this protocol involves divulging minimal information about yourself and your criminal history (if you have one). It also means *not* asking other inmates questions about themselves or their past. Having said that, *everybody* has a first time in the watch house, and you are certainly able to ask questions about the watch house and jail. *While you need to be careful not to divulge too much, it is important that you don't refuse to say anything at all about why you are in the watch house.* It looks suspicious – other inmates will begin to think the worst:

- Is he/she a 'plant' (an informer placed among other inmates to gather intelligence)?
- Is he/she an undercover police officer?
- Does his/her crime involve a sexual component?
- Was his/her offence against someone defenceless (e.g. assaulting a minor or robbing an old lady)?

Ideally you will want to come across as someone who has nothing to hide, but minds their own business. So, if you're asked, tell the truth, but not necessarily the whole truth. If you're in for assault, that's all they really need to know. Answer peripheral questions (Who'd you assault? Are they badly hurt?) but don't feel obligated to tell them everything. Answer their questions but don't ask your own – this is the best way to show you're polite, but uninterested in socialising.

Social Navigation

People with ASD learn to navigate social situations through mimicking others, rather than through intrinsic understanding. There is no more important place to do this than in prison, so start straight away, beginning at the watch house. However, *don't suddenly try to become someone different overnight.* This wouldn't work for someone highly neurotypical, and it *definitely* won't work for someone with ASD. Try to observe and follow the lead of people who appear comfortable – they will almost certainly have been there before. Along with appearing at ease in the prison setting, there may be other indicators that someone is no stranger to incarceration:

- tattoos
- a shaved head
- speaking in a confident way
- interacting with staff in a confident way
- general talk about crime and the criminal world.

Don't try to become buddy-buddy with them. It's not in your interests to appear eager to make friends while in the watch house. As mentioned earlier, people are often in a state of withdrawal from drugs, and may be agitated, slightly confused or paranoid. If this is the case, conversation is the last thing on their mind, and they could find you intrusive and irritating if you persist in trying to build a rapport.

First impressions stick: there is a high chance that at least one or two inmates who you are in the watch house with will accompany you to remand jail. As such, be very mindful of *not* making some silly, impulsive comment that could be taken out of context. It may come back to bite you.

Interacting with the Officers

Always address the watch house staff respectfully. When you are making a request (such as asking for a toothbrush, having the toilet door buzzed open or asking for them to change the TV channel), use terms such as 'chief', 'sir', 'boss', 'miss' or 'ma'am'. To get the terms correct, listen to the other inmates. *Do not call them 'mate', 'pal', 'buddy' or any other familiar term.* Other inmates may let this slide once or twice because it will be obvious you are a first-timer, but try not to make the mistake more than once. The watch house will be your first contact with other inmates – it pays to start your journey on the right foot.

Important Things to Remember About the Watch House

- You will not be in the watch house for very long (usually around five to seven days).
- The body search is non-invasive.
- Treat officers and fellow inmates with respect.
- Do *not* be overfamiliar/friendly with the officers.
- Be open about why you're there, if asked.
- Don't talk about previous crimes or ask others about theirs.
- People may be unsociable (possibly agitated or very sleepy, depending on what they are detoxing from, or just not in a frame of mind to converse).
- Make watching, listening and learning your primary focus, along with trying to be respectful and friendly.
- Be prepared for a fairly high level of discomfort and boredom.

The first thing that struck me about the watch house was its cold, almost barren feel: a lot of steel and lino-covered cement. The officers were okay, except they told us we could have two, and two only, channel changes on the TV in the morning, and two at night. Considering all they need to do is push a button, I thought this a little harsh. Having said that, I (correctly) assumed they were merely preparing me for life as a prisoner;

that is, put up and shut up. I was frustrated by the lack of comfort and, having Asperger's, I knew the fluorescent lights, cold, recycled air environment, constant echoing and lack of privacy would prove to be hard to handle. I tried to sleep as much as possible, and noticed other inmates doing the same.

I went into the watch house three times during my jail experience (because of parole releases/parole breaches), and it got a bit easier each time. The first time was seven days, and by the sixth day I was feeling exhausted (despite doing very little) and despondent. I knew they could hold me for 21 days and at that point the prospect of such a lengthy stay seemed like a bad joke. The second time was brief, about four days, and by then I had a year's jail under my belt. Although by no means an expert, I found myself answering more questions than I was asking during conversation with my fellow inmates.

Both times I could feel dope sickness starting to come over me, which, as an Aspie, made my tactile aversions even stronger. I could get my benzos but not my methadone. The third and final time, the police had come to pick me up from my parole address, so I politely asked to take my meds prior to being cuffed and put into the cop car. I had four times my dose of methadone (I had been saving one every now and again, in anticipation of my re-arrest following a drug test I knew would turn up positive). I also took a handful of Valium and Serepax. They were naïve – I mean, who is prescribed four bottles of methadone, to be consumed all at once? And why would I need a dozen Valium and half a dozen Serepax? They saw a quarter of kiffy, home-grown weed, and I convinced them it was from some herbal shop to add to tea. They swallowed that one too. On a whim, I made a run for it, but badly bruised my heel jumping down from the balcony. I didn't make it far, and I paid for it by spending the next six weeks hopping around on one leg. The cops weren't happy, but I didn't get a beat-down, so that was a plus. Thanks to the drugs I had ingested, I was out of it for about three days, to the point where other inmates in the watch house would have to wake me for meals.

Compared with jail proper, the watch house is…well, it's simply crap. It's like an endurance test. Probably not such a bad thing, since boredom will become one of your major bugbears once you get to a correctional facility. But nothing is quite as physically distressing as the watch house. For an Aspie with moderate sensory sensitivity, I can honestly say I would rather do a month in a unit in jail proper than six days in the watch house. Seriously.

CHAPTER 3

Different Types of Jails

Jails Ain't Jails

From the watch house, you will be moved to a bigger facility. It can help the inmate with ASD to know in advance what to expect from these different facilities, as although they are all jails, they all have prisoners and they all have guards, there are differences between them. This chapter gives a general overview of each.

Different Inmates, Different Jails

This chapter will make more sense if you understand the different 'types' of prisoners who make up the prison population. There are multiple reasons a person may find themselves locked up. Here's the basic rundown. They may be:

- An inmate on *remand awaiting trial*. Just as it sounds, they are locked up because the police prosecutors (or equivalent) believe they have sufficient evidence for a conviction, and the prisoner has failed in their efforts to be granted bail.

- An inmate on *remand awaiting sentencing*. The inmate has admitted to their crime during a legally taped police interview. Being on remand awaiting sentencing is only applicable to a charge that will invariably result in a custodial sentence.

- In a *reception jail* awaiting movement to a *placement jail*. This means they have either pleaded guilty or have been found guilty and are awaiting transfer to the jail where they will serve out the remainder of their sentence.

- In a *placement jail* serving their sentence. They may be in the process of applying for parole, although some prisoners will choose to do their whole sentence to avoid the arduous and slow parole process. These inmates are usually in for shorter stretches (one to four years).

- Last, but far from least, a prisoner may be in jail on a *parole violation*. In fact, most inmates in jail (be it remand, reception or placement) are there on parole violations. This is because the parole system in most countries is understaffed and draconian in nature.

Different 'Types' of Jail

As you have just read, inmates might be inside for one of several reasons. Depending on where they are on their 'journey' through the judicial system, they'll be in one of three places (four if you count the watch house at the beginning):

- *Remand jail*: designed to house people awaiting sentencing or trial.

- *Reception jail*: holds prisoners for shorter periods of time, while the authorities decide which placement jail you will be housed in.
- *Placement jail*: the jail in which you will serve out the remainder of your sentence.

The first two facilities (remand and reception) usually operate in a two-tier fashion, where they house both mainstream and protection prisoners. Obviously, these two groups are kept in separate units (segregated) and prisoner movement is highly controlled. Placement jails, on the other hand, are usually one or the other – mainstream or protection.

Please note
This isn't the case in all jurisdictions. Some placement jails do operate a two-tier system. It's just less common.

You'll spend the least time in reception jail, as it is designed to house inmates until a bed becomes available for them at a placement jail. This doesn't usually take long – about three to six weeks. The most time will be spent in placement jail, unless your crime is on the lower end of the scale. If so, you may (for example) do six months on remand, go to court and be let out that day because the judge decides six months of jail time was punishment enough. Inmates *can* be in the remand jail for relatively long periods of time, especially those with complicated legal issues. If you watch too much *Law and Order*, you're liable to think you commit a crime on Monday, get caught Tuesday, appear for trial on Wednesday and are sentenced on Thursday. Obviously, that's not true – the wheels of justice move slowly.

Remand Jail

While on remand, try to make the most of the programs and activities on offer. This helps to pass the time and distract you – very important for those with ASD. Judges look favourably upon prisoners who appear to be trying to change their behaviour for the better. Some inmates pass the time by using recreational drugs, which are more readily available in remand jails (because it's the next step from the watch house, and inmates have come in 'prepared'). *Avoid the drug scene* – inmates with ASD will be identified as easier to manipulate, and your so-called drug 'friends' will abandon you at the drop of a hat if things go bad. Drugs will be discussed in greater detail in Chapter 9.

Pros of remand jails
- More activities on offer.
- More first-timers to identify with.
- COs generally more lenient/understanding.
- Because many inmates understand their behaviour in remand jail can have an impact on sentencing, they're more likely to avoid violence.

Cons of remand jails
- First-timers sometimes think they must be super tough to survive, which can lead to fights and bullying behaviour.
- More drugs equal more violence, along with frequent cell searches and lockdowns.
- Prisons get 'harder' further down the line, so remand jail can lull some prisoners into a false sense of security. Avoid this by *always* remaining vigilant.

While on remand, I met a very eclectic bunch of people. There were people there who had gotten one too many drunk in public charges, all the way up to alleged murderers and everything in between. One guy I knew had been charged with murder, but was pushing to have the charge downgraded to manslaughter. Because of his seemingly endless adjournments, and with the Director of Public Prosecutions taking their sweet time, this individual was on remand for almost four years. By the time he went to court for sentencing on manslaughter charges, which he had been offered in exchange for a guilty plea, it was almost time to go home. He had essentially done his time, all in remand. Obviously, his case was the exception to the rule, but it illustrates the elastic nature of remand jails.

Reception Jail

Reception jails are often plagued with higher levels of violence. This is because of the revolving-door nature of the facility. When inmates don't feel settled, and don't have time to form meaningful friendships, it creates an air of 'every man for himself'. Also, visits are more difficult to organise: because inmates come and go so fast, they don't have time to organise clearance for their people. This is detrimental to the collective vibe within the facility for two reasons:

1. Inmates may not have visits to look forward to.
2. Most of the illicit substances in jail come from visits.

When the drug supply runs low, the addicts become agitated and potentially dangerous. Medical issues, such as access to the correct medication, physical problems or mental health concerns are treated with a band-aid approach, because staff don't expect to have to deal with inmates for long. Prisoners with ASD should have their diagnosis recognised while in the remand or place-ment jail, not reception jail (provided you want to disclose your ASD – see Chapter 5 for more on this).

Pros of reception jails
- You won't be there for long.
- Because of the relatively short duration of your stay, other inmates may not have time to sense you are 'different'.

Cons of reception jails
- Higher levels of violence because of rapid prisoner movement.
- Very few activities on offer.
- Indifferent COs.
- Comparatively poor medical care, especially regarding mental health.

The time I spent at the reception jail was, in many ways, the most challenging. I know I'm not the only one who feels this way; the consensus among inmates is that, second only to the watch house, reception jails are the worst environment to be housed in.

At one point, I was asked to provide a urine sample. I wasn't worried about testing positive, because I wasn't using. However, I have trouble pissing with two men standing about a metre away. I managed to squeeze out a few drops, but it didn't reach the line on the cup, the one that gives a preliminary indication of drug use. So, the screw goes, 'Well, sorry, but we're going to count this as a refusal to supply. As you know, that counts as a dirty.'

I wasn't about to take this lying down, so I said, 'But you can still send the small amount to the lab for testing. They only need a drop.'

The screw looked at me for a second, then promptly flushed the contents of the cup down the toilet. I was fucking furious but kept it to myself. On top of that, when I went back out into the yard I was grilled, and almost bashed, by three big scary dudes, because they assumed I had taken 20 minutes dogging on other inmates. They didn't want to hear the truth: that I simply had trouble pissing while two screws were breathing down my neck. So, on top of almost being bashed, and having my reputation questioned by fellow inmates, I unjustly received a breach for 'failing to provide a urine sample', despite the fact that I did provide one. The whole episode cost me about three months more time inside, when I could have been out on parole.

Placement Jail

Placement jails are generally easier to live in than reception or remand jails. This is because inmates feel 'settled' – knowing there will be no more movement unless it is requested. Some inmates are in a placement jail for years, even decades, so treat your surroundings as if you're in their home (at least until you get settled – and even then, always show respect). Staff behave differently too – when COs are seeing the same faces day in, day out, they start to see a person rather than a number. Drugs are harder to get, which, hopefully, will mean nothing to you. Drugs are *not* your friend in jail. Violence in placement jails can be more brutal, as it may be perpetrated by inmates serving long sentences. When someone has 14 years before they can even *apply* for parole, the thought of spending a month in solitary confinement for bashing another inmate is little deterrent.

On the upside, placement jails have less *frequent* incidences of violence: by the time inmates are housed in placement jails, they know the 'unofficial' rules, so fights are rarely misunderstandings that flare into violence – the essence of most prison fights. Placement jails have more full-time staff dedicated to helping prisoners cope with mental health problems, because the facility has a vested interest in keeping inmates calm and cooperative. For inmates with ASD, it is in a placement jail that they can expect to have their diagnosis treated with the degree of sincerity it warrants. Placement jails may also offer government-subsidised education. Some inmates obtain high school certificates and even undergraduate degrees. Access to education and other activities will be discussed in Chapter 11.

Residential accommodation
Placement jails can sometimes offer housing in what's known as 'residential accommodation' ('res'). This is part of the jail where inmates are not confined to individual units, but rather they live in smaller, separate blocks, with four to six inmates apiece. These units are scattered across a large area, and inmates can move around freely. Inmates have their own key to their cells, although there is a locking mechanism that means you can't open your door 24 hours a day. They too are locked down around 5.00–6.00 pm and you are allowed out from around 7.00 am.

Pros of placement jails
- Inmates are more settled and therefore more relaxed.
- Social hierarchies are more established, so less violence.
- COs are more respectful.
- Mental health issues are taken seriously.
- Applying for tertiary education is a bit easier.
- Making friends is easier as there is less prisoner movement.

Cons of placement jails

- When violence *does* occur, it can be more brutal.
- COs, while easier to get along with, are tougher. If you break the rules, they are quick to restore order, using whatever force necessary.
- Long-term inmates see placement jails as their home; thus, 'ownership' feelings can make inmates pedantic and inflexible.
- Placement jail is the end of the road. If you make enemies here, the only place left to go is (possibly) the special needs unit (SNU), or to protection.

Better cooking equipment and more frequent access to the communal gym and oval are also available in 'res'. It may sound like a comparatively good deal, but 'res' probably *won't* suit inmates with ASD. Why?

A standard unit has 50 men, give or take a few depending on prisoner movement and whether inmates are being 'doubled-up' (one cell, two men). Residential, on the other hand, is home to literally *hundreds* of prisoners. More inmates means significantly more social interaction, so for someone with ASD, this can prove to be a drain on their mental resources. Making just one mistake can mean the entire 'res' population could turn on you, and (as mentioned earlier), social mistakes can follow you around. Making a mistake and having 50 inmates know about it isn't great, but it's an awful lot better than *500* inmates knowing. For inmates with ASD, 'res' is *not* a good idea.

What struck me when arriving at placement jail was the comparatively calm atmosphere, at least compared with the shithole reception jail I had been in for the previous five weeks. It was a nice surprise. Inmates had their established cliques, which was fine with me because, as those with Asperger's understand, I was quite content to sit quietly and read a book. I started working out on day two, and my well-developed physique elicited a few genuine compliments.

Initially everything was fine, but it wasn't long before the bully types homed in on me, like a shark smelling blood in the water. There was no physical abuse, but when my fellow inmates found out that I would jump when unexpectedly poked in the ribs, this became an endless source of amusement. My sensitivity to touch was shamelessly exploited. I didn't fight back, although in retrospect I sometimes wish I had. Having said that, would it really have been a good idea? What if I had been punched, fallen and hit my head on the concrete? I often wonder about that, even these days. I went with my gut, ignored the lightweight taunting, and focused on training and reading. But the relentless, low-level bullying did get to me. By the time I was granted parole, four and a half months later, I had developed a nervous twitch in my left eye. It disappeared within a couple of weeks of being out of there, but will forever remain a stark reminder of just how stressed I got in placement jail (at least in the run-of-the-mill units).

CHAPTER 4

Transport

Why Address Transportation?

Transportation is the only time during incarceration you will
be *forced* to be in very close proximity to another inmate. The
style of transportation varies from country to country. In the US
they use buses that can sit 52 inmates, with just two guards to
keep order. If there's a fight, they drive post-haste to the nearest
correctional facility. This can be up to half an hour away. The
COs do not attempt to stop the fight. Fifty-two against two, even
with the prisoners shackled, aren't good odds.

The Prison Bus

Transportation is unavoidable, as prisoners cannot be kept in the
watch house for long. Space is continually an issue, so they want
to get you in, process you and get you on a transport to remand
jail post-haste. Transporting inmates is taken very seriously by
correctional departments. You may have seen a movie where

somehow, during transit from one facility to another, prisoners either take control of the transport or a third party intervenes, freeing them to go and terrorise the populace. This is unlikely to be an issue. However, because inmates are technically in the public domain while in transit, the COs don't mess around. Be cooperative and patient.

Please note
This book is written from experiences in Australian jails. We have a slightly different mode of transportation – only in the sense that the buses are smaller. Irrespective of *exactly* what sort of vehicle you're in, the advice remains applicable. Because of the difficulty people with ASD have with socialising, this book will hopefully provide helpful advice, regardless of where you are doing time (and how you get there from the watch house).

Potential Issues with Transportation

All inmates dislike transportation. The inmate with ASD may find it particularly challenging for several reasons:

- Inmates are handcuffed for the entire duration of the trip.
- The space in which you sit is quite small, so there is little room to move.
- For economic reasons, transports are usually full – sharing your little rectangular box with someone is almost guaranteed.

If your handcuffs are too tight, you can politely ask the CO to loosen them. If you find yourself sitting next to a particularly unappealing inmate, forget about asking to move – this isn't primary school, and, besides, the inmate may take offence, something you want to avoid.

Why Inmates Find Themselves in Transit

- They're required to attend a court hearing in person.
- They are being moved from one facility to another.
- They're being driven to hospital for non-urgent medical issues (ambulances attend emergencies in jail).
- They're going to the funeral of an immediate family member.

Please note
Not all jurisdictions will allow inmates to attend funerals, and those that do require the money for transportation to be raised by family and friends.

Coping with Transportation

Journeys can be long, so talking can help pass the time. For the inmate with ASD, this prospect may cause anxiety, and small talk can be tiring. However, ignoring other inmates looks rude. Making a good impression, even if it's with only one person, is in your interest. When sharing small spaces, be yourself – but remember:

- If you're contesting the charges, avoid revealing specific details. Explain the nature of your charges and other basic details. *Don't refuse to talk* – people will think you have something to hide, like charges involving children.

- Be reciprocal. Ask about why they're in transit but be subtle. Ask general questions (what unit they're in, is it okay there, etc.) You *don't* want to appear to be fishing for information regarding crimes.
- Police can put undercover operatives inside jails, including transports. Always remember – think before you speak!

Please note
Conversations in transports are recorded, so always keep this at the back of your mind.

As for social interaction, not much will be expected of you. If the person next to you seems insistent on talking, but you would prefer silence, respond with small, polite responses but don't ask them questions. Hopefully, they will soon get the message.

I was on a prison transport going from placement jail to a court house some 50-odd kilometres away. I was facing charges relating to drug-driving, which I had committed while out on parole. I had driven my mother's car back from a friend, somehow miraculously avoiding any traffic accidents (I have almost no memory of the journey), only to crash into a pole in my parents' housing estate – literally 500 metres from my destination.

As this offence occurred while on parole, and because the wheels of justice turn slowly, I didn't end up facing court until after I had returned to jail on a parole breach. No one had been hurt in the crash, so if I seem flippant about it, that's why.

At this placement jail, they woke me with plenty of time

to spare – 3.45 am. They buzzed my intercom, telling me they would come to get me in 40 minutes. They did – then I was left in a holding cell for two and a half hours.

A nice guy from res was my travelling companion. By this stage in my incarceration, I had decided to use my Asperger's diagnosis to move into the SNU. When asked what unit I came from, I simply said 'two'. He assumed I meant G2, a 'normal' unit. He asked me if I knew this guy and that guy, so I explained I had only been there a couple of weeks and was still learning names. He was okay with that. You cross paths with literally hundreds of other inmates during your time in jail, and remembering names isn't always easy.

We dozed while on the journey there. On the way back from court, my travelling companion and I were a bit more lively, keen to get 'home' and into our cells for dinner, then some comfortable sleep. We chatted about a lot of things on the way back, animated because the long day was over, and we had both gotten satisfactory results in court. We got off the transport, were led to medical to get our PM meds and have a brief search carried out. Then the CO said, 'Which one of you is from S2? Have we got someone from S2 here?'

'Uh, yeah,' I said a bit gingerly. 'That's me.'

My new buddy didn't seem too impressed. I had technically broken a code – the code of being honest about what unit you are in or what units you've been in. But I didn't give a shit. What was he gonna do? Attack me with four screws around? Besides, I had only a few months left and knew the chances of coming face to face with him again were minimal. I got back to the unit, had my dinner, read some of my book and fell into a deep, peaceful sleep. I never saw this old mate again.

CHAPTER 5

The Big Question

What Question?

This book provides information and advice to help those with ASD cope with jail. But there's the significant issue of whether you:

- tell the relevant parties about your ASD diagnosis, in the hope it will provide access to suitable accommodation and treatment
- keep the diagnosis 'in your back pocket' and see how you fare in the regular units. If things turn ugly, you have the option of divulging your diagnosis, to be accommodated in a more appropriate setting.

Whatever your initial position is, think before you commit. You can always wait and mention your diagnosis later, but you can't suddenly make it disappear once you've told the authorities – who may put you in an SNU or equivalent without even asking, because they're covering themselves from a legal standpoint.

People reading this will invariably have contrasting viewpoints about whether to let the jail know or not, and both have merit. Having said that, factor in the following:

- Social rules in jail are complex and fluid.
- Unspoken rules can be bent but not broken – breaking them once could cause serious trouble.
- Sometimes, rules seem to run counter to *other* rules.
- Socialisation in jail is likely to be difficult for inmates with ASD.

For the socially inept, jail can be a lion's den. Viewing your diagnosis as a 'golden ticket' to the SNU is completely understandable. However, not all jails will offer an SNU. In this case, they usually have an equivalent facility to cope with your needs – you're not the first inmate to have mental health issues, and you won't be the last.

Why Going to the SNU Can Be a Good Choice

People with ASD prefer social dynamics to be simple, honest and straightforward – the opposite of prison culture. For inmates with ASD, this grey area is a minefield – if you're in a normal unit, and 'get out of line', sometimes just once, you can be assaulted. SNUs abide by the same codes, but 'punishment' for infractions is far more reasonable, and violence is used as a last resort. Keep in mind that, although the SNU is more relaxed, repeated violations will result in the inmate being hurt. Apart from the two main points mentioned above, *SNUs are still jail*. The contents of this book are applicable to both SNUs and regular units.

The first time I saw just how crazy jail can be was when an older gentleman entered our unit from the unit next door. The screws had to move him because he was threatened with a bashing. His mistake?

Three years prior, he had been in the same unit, and had accidently walked on a mopped floor. By walk, I mean one step. Just by chance, the mopper was also in the same unit this second time around, and he recognised the older gentleman. So, the mopper gathered up his boys and threatened the older gentleman with a bashing. For the older man, it was a matter of stay and get bashed, or request movement at the risk of being labelled 'a bailer' (as in 'he's bailing because he's scared'). The older gentleman made the 'choice' to leave. It saddens me that when people are already under duress, some scumbags just can't help but twist the knife.

How to Decide Which Way to Go

Put simply, it comes down to this:

- Are you familiar with 'the street' (usually through addiction)?
- Do you know 'street' criminals (not paedophiles or white-collar criminals)?
- Do you understand street/jail vernacular?
- Are you a proficient fighter?
- Are you prepared to fight, regardless of whom you're fighting?

If you answered 'yes' to three or more of these questions, you will likely fare okay in regular units. If you answered 'no' to *all* of them, then you should put serious thought into applying for the SNU. Jails in developed nations should recognise ASD as genuinely detrimental to your safety, and because of their duty of care to every inmate, you could argue that it's your *right* to live in a safe environment. Before deciding, consider the following.

Being open about your diagnosis can help you in the following ways:

- Access to the SNU.
- Being deemed unsuitable to share a cell with another inmate, so you can get *proper* downtime.
- Quicker access to mental health services.
- Access to specialised material, such as books about ASD or puzzle books for mental stimulation, etc.
- Telling fellow inmates about ASD is not necessarily a bad thing. All inmates are people, with hopes, dreams, fears and vulnerabilities. Hence, their reaction may well be one of interest and support.
- If other inmates know, it may provide you with some leeway if you break or violate 'the prison code', at least to an extent. They are unlikely, however, to turn the other cheek if you tell on somebody and say, 'I can't help it – it's my ASD'. That won't wash.
- The parole board may factor in your ASD if/when you need to make a parole application. They will understand that life for you in jail may well have been negatively affected by ASD.

The Argument *Against* Telling Corrective Services

Even developed, progressive nations don't provide first-rate medical care in jails – after all, we're just 'crims'. Most people will never see the inside of a jail, so they care little about what goes on in there. With no political incentive to improve conditions, at least not rapidly, you may find yourself fighting a losing battle to have your diagnosis recognised. For the inmate with ASD, this is a frustrating reality of life behind bars. In a better world, jails would make catering to the mental health needs of prisoners a priority. In a perfect world, there would be ASD-specific units in all jails. But even if there *were* SNUs or ASD-specific units in every jail, it would be presumptuous to assume every inmate with a diagnosis would want to go there. A balanced approach is needed when discussing any issue of significance.

Being open about your diagnosis can hinder you in the following ways:

- There is a likely chance you will be sharing the SNU with an eclectic mix of inmates, including:
    - schizophrenics
    - inmates with acquired brain injuries (ABIs)
    - inmates who have brain damage from excessive alcohol or drug consumption
    - inmates who have significantly below-average intelligence
    - other inmates with ASD
    - inmates with bipolar disorder
    - inmates with personality disorders.
- SNUs have the undertone of a psychiatric facility, just not as overt. If this is something that might bother you, please take it into consideration.
- If you want to get drugs or homebrew alcohol to cope, there is almost no chance of getting it in the SNU. (*Having said that, it is a very bad idea to get mixed up in the illicit drug scene, which includes alcohol. Drug use behind bars will be discussed in greater length in Chapter 9. But remember, it is not a good idea, even in the comparative calm of the SNU.*)

- SNU inmates are looked down upon by inmates from other units, as they may see it as a 'soft' option – they think you're 'faking' to get an easy ride.
- This may curtail your confidence to utilise programs/ activities where you may interact with people from regular units. Things like:
  - oval/gym time (units often go in pairs)
  - education activities (these are held in separate buildings within the prison)
  - work – often inmates who choose to work in the kitchen, laundry or gardening crews will work with people from 'normal' units
  - visits
  - going to medical.
- SNUs sometimes house inmates who don't have a mental health condition but have said or done something 'wrong' in another unit. For their safety they're housed in the SNU. Nine times out of ten this is fine. Sometimes, however, the inmate realises the dynamic is different, and they start intimidating fellow inmates. These hypocrites bailed from a 'hard' unit, ended up in a 'soft' one and then become bullies. Fortunately, they never last long – the authorities move them on, or they're driven out by the inmates (even SNU inmates have their pride/limited patience).

Deciding

As mentioned before, you can keep your diagnosis as a 'back-up' plan should you find yourself being bullied in the normal units. This book will explain the lifestyle, unwritten rules, dangers and warning signs to look out for in the 'normal' units. If, after reading the book, you feel you can cope, then perhaps you could start in a normal unit and go from there. On the other hand, if you are quite far along the spectrum (meaning your ASD is quite pronounced), or you simply want to make your time in jail easier and you couldn't care less what inmates from 'normal' units think, then apply ASAP to be transferred to the SNU.

If there appears to be no such thing as an SNU at the jail you are sent to, don't stress – stressing never helped anybody! There will be a way, if you and your jailers work together, to find you an environment that is safe but not completely segregated. Inmates should only be in complete segregation as punishment – putting an inmate with ASD into an environment like that is very unethical, and they would know this. All jails will have inmates who, for a variety of reasons, need to be segregated from the alpha male behaviour of 'normal' units.

I spent about two-thirds of my prison time in normal, run-of-the-mill units. I did encounter problems, including violence, which in hindsight were directly related to my Asperger's. I would inadvertently break some unspoken rule or say the wrong thing at the wrong time. This didn't happen often and, luckily, I suffered injuries no worse than bruising, swelling and abrasions. I'm not a tough guy. I hate fighting. I hate violence. I hate seeing people fight. I hate the sound of fists hitting bodies. It's something of a myth that you must be willing to fight if someone 'offers you out'. What is more important is keeping your mouth shut if you get attacked. Even though there was low-level bullying, I wasn't considered a threat because other inmates could sense two things: one, I was an experienced (and knowledgeable) drug user; and two, they could tell I understood the code of not talking to the screws if something went down.

However, I chose to do my last ten months in the SNU because I was sick of the low-level bullying and harassment I had received in 'normal' units. Those fuckers can smell weakness, and they picked on me for whatever reason it is that people pick on people. Personally, I think the adage is true – bullies are inadequate pieces of shit desperate to prove something, or right some perceived wrong from years ago. Who knows for sure? All I know is asking to be moved to the SNU was a very, very good decision. Here's an example of how things roll in normal units.

I was in a 'Bronx' (tough) unit, in one of the tougher jails in the state and a placement jail, so it had dangerous men serving long sentences for violent offences. I was lightly picked on – nothing I couldn't handle. But it started to wear thin. They would do things like sneak up behind me and poke my ribs, causing a very overt involuntary reaction. This seemed to be endlessly entertaining. They would ask hilarious and clever questions like: 'So does your boyfriend miss you?' But I wasn't assaulted, I wasn't yelled at and I ignored the jibes – focusing instead on working out and reading and helping people with their parole applications. People may think, 'Why on earth would you help these people who taunt you so?' Well, first, not all the inmates were obnoxious. Some were fine. Some were good guys. In fact, most of the unit just ignored me. In a 52-man unit, there were maybe 10, 12 people who regularly poked me, or accused me of spying when I was sitting alone reading. But one can only take so much. Here's an example of where my Asperger's got the better of me.

I snapped one day. I mouthed off at the unofficial 'head' of the unit, the inmate no one messes with. He was shouting over the wall in the exercise yard to the yard next door, organising a drug deal. He said something about me trying to spy and accused me of being a dog, even though I was just cutting laps and he came into my space. I lost it – told him to fuck off and stop being such an obnoxious C%$% and so on.

Well, it ended badly, with me on the ground, blood gushing from my nose. But the other inmates rallied around me (partly because they knew I had been right to try to stand up for myself) but more because they didn't want the unit to get locked down. There had been several fights over the last month or so, a couple bad enough that the screws had to call in the turtles. The powers-that-be had had enough of us knuckle-heads, so we knew we would get locked down for a couple of days if they had to deal with more blood.

Someone brought me a clean shirt from the spares in the laundry, tissues to stem the bleeding from the nose and water to wash the blood off me and the concrete. The screws had no idea, until, of course, about a day and a half later when the bruising became quite prominent. Subtly, one of them asked if I felt safe, or if I needed to bail from the unit. I told him, 'No, all is sorted.' The screw was cool about it too. He said it very softly, and while he was 'looking up' something on the computer. He did this so other inmates couldn't accuse me of dobbing or answering questions.

There is protocol, so the screw must report injuries to his senior and it goes up to the area manager. About two days after the incident, they took me from the unit into their office area and asked me what happened. I told them I fell into a fence, and never deviated from that story. Eventually they gave up and said, 'Well, just make sure you and the fence don't have any more problems.' Even they seemed happy that I was letting it go. Nobody likes a dog.

I got back into the unit and, although no one said anything, they were all waiting to see if the screws would approach the *attacker. When they didn't, and two, three more days went by and old mate wasn't questioned, and no cells were ramped, it was all over and done with. I earned respect by keeping my mouth shut.*

I got out on parole after four months in that shitty unit, and got my diagnosis. I had always suspected I was on the spectrum, but never confirmed it. After it came back that I did have ASD…well, everything kinda…fell into place. It was a revelation. I knew I would be going back to jail – I still had a year to go on my sentence and I was struggling with drugs – a breach was inevitable. But I made myself a promise – I would use my diagnosis as leverage for an easier prison life.

Part 2
Practical Jail

The second part of this book looks at the practical side of jail – the who, where, what, when and how of living behind bars. Naturally, not *everything* about jail is covered, but rather the more important parts (like visits and organising financial support). Knowing in advance what to expect, at least to a degree, should help reduce anxiety through illumination of the unknown. Humans often fear what they *don't* know more than bad things they do. Not that this section of the book looks at issues in a good/bad fashion – it simply tells it like it is. How one responds to the information will vary.

As mentioned before: forewarned is forearmed. For those with ASD, forewarning is especially pertinent. People with ASD don't cope well with surprises, so the focus of this section is to provide the reader with an understanding of what to expect once they arrive.

Information is tailored to help inmates with ASD. Hopefully, after reading this section, jail will seem less like an abstract concept with connotations of fear, and more like another bridge to cross in the journey of life.

CHAPTER 6

So, You've Arrived

First Things First

Remember – you are strong. You are unique. You matter just as much as anybody else. You are not a number – you are a person, and only you can allow your spirit to be broken. Jail can be tough. Jail can be confusing. Jail can be dangerous. But stand your ground, and keep your eyes focused on the light at the end of the tunnel. Talk to people outside jail for support. Moreover, use some of the techniques this book will teach you, like watch, listen and learn, and see no evil, hear no evil, speak no evil. If you do this, and do it consistently, you may be surprised just how relatively 'easy' jail can be.

What to Expect Upon Arrival

As stressed in the disclaimer, this is a general guide. Different jails have differing protocol, but the deviations are likely to be minimal. Upon arrival, expect the following:

- Another search of you, basically the same as the watch house (see Chapter 2).
- A shower – these are not voluntary.
- Clothes changed from watch house clothing to jail clothing.
- Confirmation of the property (e.g. wallet, watch, shoes, etc.) taken from you when you were arrested or sentenced, to ensure everything has arrived in jail with you. All these belongings will be safely stored and returned to you on your release.
- Your photo will be taken for your prison ID. This allows you to be visually identified while moving around the jail. The ID card will be issued to you a bit later down the track. Generally, these cards are *not* allowed to be kept by the prisoner. You will be asked to hand them to the COs when you get to your unit, and they will be given to you temporarily when you need to move around the centre (like going to medical and back from your unit).
- A brief, one-on-one discussion with a psychologist – *if you have decided to let the jail system know about your Asperger's, this discussion is very important – it will be the mental health team that will help you, and this will be your first interaction with them.*

Having said that, keep the discussion as brief as possible. You will be processed as a group, and your group can only move as fast as the slowest member. Try to be succinct with nurses, psychologists and other staff for two reasons:

1. The inmates you arrived with are bored and frustrated too – they won't appreciate you spending 45 minutes with the psychologist when everyone else took five. If you are telling the psychologist about having ASD and your desire

to be in the SNU (or equivalent), you don't need to labour the point. They will understand your eagerness and follow up on it – that's their job.

2. In jail, *everything* moves more slowly, and inmates with ASD experience frustration differently to their neurotypical counterparts. Put simply – be patient. Even if it means running your 'patience tanks' almost empty. Use self-soothing techniques, don't complain too much (all of you are in the same boat), and don't try to engage another inmate in extended conversation (it's unlikely they'll feel much like talking). Just grin and bear it. By the time it's over, you'll wonder why it frustrated you so much at the time. And above all else remember – you're being processed into a first world jail, not Auschwitz.

The Final Part of Processing

After you have all been showered, searched, spoken to by the psychologist and so forth, you will be issued with a *bed pack*, which usually consists of the following:

- bedding
- a note book
- a pen
- some envelopes
- toothpaste
- a toothbrush

- a couple of razors
- soap
- two sets of clothes
- a laundry bag for washing
- a pillow.

Upon arrival, prisons offer inmates the opportunity to get (on 'credit') a limited selection of items from the canteen, or 'buy-up' list. The cost will temporarily send your prison account 'into the red'. However, as soon as money goes *into* your account you will pay back the debt, and any money you receive thereafter is all yours. Money goes into your account in the following ways:

- Your people send you money (the term 'your people' is used frequently in jail as a generic term encompassing anyone who may be on the phone list, who writes to you, sends you money or is generally there to support you).
- The 'hygiene allowance' provided by the government.
- Money from working in a jail job.

'Canteen/commissary' (or 'buy-ups' as they're called in Australia) and how prison accounts work are discussed in Chapter 12. Prisons that allow smoking will likely issue cigarettes at this point. If you are a non-smoker, decline the offer. *Be wary of being talked into getting cigarettes for somebody else – this may be seen as a weakness and may start an unwanted pattern. If pushed (metaphorically), say you have no one on the outside to put money into your account, and you need all the money you can get. Be firm. It is very important to stay firm and assertive, even though you may want to revert to an attitude of submissiveness 'to avoid trouble'. You will avoid future trouble if you can stand your ground from the very beginning. This is one of the most significant pieces of advice contained in this book – remember it and do your best to implement it if/when the time comes.*

Prison Number and PIN

When you first came into serious contact with the law, an identification code will have been allocated to you. When you first arrive, you will be given details of your number. You will memorise it quickly, as you use it often. The PIN part ensures you and you alone can access your phone account. People can theoretically get your prison number because sometimes they get written on the COs' whiteboard (not just yours, usually a bunch of people, like inmates who are enrolled in a class which is being held that day). For information on how to use the phone system, see Chapter 12.

Medical Processing

Finally, you will be taken to medical for a brief once-over by a nurse. It's best to mention your diagnosis to the psychologist when you first come in rather than to the nurse, because you may not have as much privacy as you do in the psychologist's office. All prisoners will see the doctor at some point in their first month in jail, usually sooner rather than later.

If, for some reason, your medicinal needs were not met in the watch house, now is the time to talk firmly (but politely – always politely) to the nurse. You will be in the remand jail for long enough to justify getting your medicines and diagnoses officially recognised. The ins and outs of medical treatment will be discussed in the next chapter.

Dietary Requirements

During the intake process, you may be asked to fill out a form regarding dietary needs. Prisons cater to medical, religious or cultural requirements. If this hasn't been addressed, and you do have a dietary issue, talk to the nurse regarding your concerns.

Reception Call

Once you have settled into your unit, you will be given a 'reception call'. These allow you to call someone and let them know where you are (if you didn't make a call from the watch house), that you are okay and may possibly need some money to be sent to you, so you can continue to make calls. Reception calls are made in front of a CO, and it's best to keep them short. How to make calls from the prison phones (and put money into your phone account) is discussed in Chapter 11.

The Social Side

So far, this chapter has explained what to expect upon arrival from a practical point of view. But it's the social side of prison that is particularly relevant for those on the spectrum. So, the next part of this chapter is devoted to social conduct.

First Impressions

Once something is said, it can't be 'unsaid', which brings to mind the old saying 'if you don't have anything nice to say, don't say anything at all'. More specifically, for someone new to prison – if you haven't got something that *needs* to be said, don't say anything at all. Just watch, listen and learn. It's the best thing you can do. On that note, it's okay to admit you are nervous. Almost everyone is nervous when new to jail, and as a first-timer, you are likely to get sympathy and support from the seasoned prisoners and empathy from the other first-timers. Also, it's very unlikely you will be the only inmate in the unit who's on the spectrum. ASD equals anxiety, anxiety can equal drug use/addiction, addiction can lead to crime and crime can lead to prison.

Expecting Change

People with ASD generally dislike change – something as innocuous as a change in breakfast regime can have a detrimental effect on mood. This book is designed to minimise the severity of your reaction to change, by explaining in advance how jail works, both practically and socially. Knowledge is power – having an understanding of jail prior to stepping foot in one should help offset the upset in routine and give you an inner sense of fortitude.

Flexibility and Routine

Obviously, jail will be a new routine. ASD and flexibility aren't exactly synonymous, but in jail it is imperative you're flexible and cooperative. Initially, COs, known as 'screws' by inmates, see you as just another prisoner, little more than a number. As time goes on they see your face more frequently. Eventually, you will become less a number and more a person. That's why it can pay to wait until you feel a bit more 'settled in' before informing them of your ASD (if that's what you plan to do). You may find you like the way normal units run, in which case there's no real need to go the SNU. There are inmates with ASD who are in the 'tough' units, have friends in there and get by just fine.

Mimicking

People with ASD cope by *mimicking* the behaviour they see around them. They do this irrespective of whether they are aware of it. However, try not to mimic all the behaviour displayed by inmates. Aim to emulate the behaviour of *seasoned prisoners* – prisoners who have amassed a considerable amount of jail time. Seasoned prisoners are often identifiable simply by the 'vibe' they give off. Just like in the watch house, look for indicators of extended stints inside:

- Tattoos – particularly on the legs. Also, tattoos that appear to be 'unprofessional' – faded, half-finished, etc. These are tattoos that have probably been drawn during a previous stretch inside.
- A strong build.
- A wiry build can be a sign too – they may be a stimulant user on the outside.
- A shaved head or an 'aggressive' haircut – such as having a ponytail but shaving the rest of the head.
- The way they move – confident, familiar.
- The way they talk – prisoners often speak in a unique way, but the actual sound can vary from state to state and jail to jail.
- The way they address other people, both fellow inmates and the COs.
- What they talk about – e.g. other prisons they have been in, people they may know in the jail, general crime talk, etc.

Basically, it won't be difficult to identify these people. Remember – *watch, listen and learn.*

So, What Are You In For?

Be careful when it comes to asking other inmates what they are in jail for. You will be curious, just as they will be curious about you. If an inmate *does* ask you, tell them the truth, but not the whole story from beginning to end. If you're a chatty person, just keep it to a minimum until you are settled (and even then, try to avoid dominating conversations). If you seem completely uninterested in *other* inmates' crimes, they could misinterpret that as you behaving in a manner that you think will lessen the chance of *them* asking *you* about your crime – and you never want to look like you aren't prepared to talk about your crime. Inmates will be all over that one, desperate to find out if you're hiding anything. Talking a lot about your crime could also look suspicious: he 'doth protest too much'. Although your average prisoner may not think in Shakespearean language, they might start wondering – why does this person seem desperate to talk about their crime? Are they trying to convince me because it's a lie? Better to keep it short and sweet. When asked, tell them the actual charge(s) against you. If they seem interested and ask other questions, seeking more detail, give it to them, but don't carry on about it. Only elaborate on details inmates seem interested in. If someone has asked you, that's a green light to ask them. As time progresses, and prison becomes more familiar, you will learn to gauge if/when and how to ask that question, if you feel the need to ask it at all.

The Arbitrary Moral Compass

Some offences are looked down upon by inmates, such as child-related crime, scamming or stealing from the disabled or elderly, and stealing from one's family. The best policy is to (again!) watch, listen and learn.

....

In the first-timer's unit at the remand jail, I noticed some crimes were considered more acceptable than others. This makes sense. Even the most liberal, open-minded person will find it hard to respect someone who has raped and killed a child. Of course, the perpetrator of such a crime would be in protection. That was just an extreme example to illustrate my point. Mainstream (and protection, I can only assume) have a kind of unwritten 'severity' chart, where certain crimes are frowned upon while others are accepted. This self-imposed 'severity' barometer seemed to be quite dynamic and, for an Aspie, sometimes quite illogical.

For example, if a man robs a house (while the occupant is out), gets caught and the owner turns out to be elderly, he can expect trouble if he ends up in jail, even though he had no idea the house he was robbing was owned by an elderly person. Meanwhile, it's considered quite okay to have a pretty girl go into a nice bar or club, find the wealthiest looking sucker to buy her a drink, check he's got plenty of cash in his wallet when he goes to pay for it, gulp down the drink, then ask if he 'wants to go someplace a bit quieter'. She leads him out of the club, around the corner to her co-offenders who then proceed to beat the man unconscious and steal all his possessions. Broken bones? No drama. Permanent scarring? Who cares? Brain damage for the rest of his life? Well, he should have been more careful!

These aren't hypothetical situations. These examples are based on real events. The house-robber was given a hard time, and the men who bashed a guy (four on one) into a coma – nothing. Just some more inmates doing their time.

Eye Contact

Now you are among other inmates in a setting larger than the watch house, it's pertinent to address an issue that will be with you from beginning to end – eye contact. People with ASD can sometimes find making eye contact difficult. This is arguably one area where you will be helped rather than hindered by your ASD. As most people know, especially men, prolonged eye contact is a clear sign of confrontation. It won't take long to master the 'art' of making eye contact without being confrontational. Difficult to describe but easy to imitate, neutral eye contact means 'skimming' over the eyes of other inmates. Find the balance between appearing relaxed and at ease, while not looking arrogant or nonchalant. While it may sound tricky, it's not. Again, look to the seasoned prisoners and how they do it. If someone thinks you are 'staring them down', you can avoid conflict by saying, 'Shit, sorry. I thought you were a guy who used to live in my street,' or 'I have no problem with you. I thought you were someone else.' Don't try to avoid eye contact entirely, as it might attract predators or give people the wrong impression about how you are coping. When questioned by a CO, avoiding eye contact can be misinterpreted as guilt or an attempt to be evasive. Don't expend too much energy worrying about eye contact – you will learn as you go.

Tips to Help the Newcomer

Here are some key points to remember:

- You are not alone.
- Others have gone before you and survived.

- *Do not* believe what you have seen on TV and in the movies.
- Ask yourself: Am I okay *right now*? Am I free of immediate threats? Have I got food in my stomach? Do I have warm clothes on? Because there are *always* people worse off than you. Always.
- You will be *leaving*, not arriving, one day.
- You are paying your debt to society.

I remember getting off the prison transport, and being surrounded by steel and cement and razor wire, but feeling a million dollars because I could finally feel a breeze on my face and breathe normal air. After a week of recycled air in the watch house, it felt wonderful. I would never have thought I'd appreciate a fresh breeze so much. But jail does that to you. Every cloud has a silver lining, and one of these is to help you appreciate the little things. Truly mastering this skill will get you a long way in life generally, and is especially helpful on the inside.

While sitting in little holding cells all day, I met a range of people. They could tell it was my first time inside, but they were very supportive. I even helped one of them write his parole letter that afternoon. I didn't feel threatened at all at this point, especially since I already knew some of the jail lingo from my associates on the outside. Also, I was there for the same reason so many are: drug addiction. Well, specifically I was there for armed robbery, but my crimes were committed because of drug addiction. Having something in common with my fellow inmates, even if it led to cravings, seemed important to me. I suppose, in retrospect, it was important.

I had no trouble whatsoever during my time in the remand jail. One thing that had put my mind at ease considerably was what the psychologist had told me during intake. I sat down, and he asked how I was. I told him I was nervous. Then he said to me, 'I know from your file here it's your first time inside. I want to make something very clear from the get-go: forget what you think you know about jail from movies and television.' He looked at me closely. 'People are not raped. There is no one here called Bubba who's coming to get you. I have never encountered a rape victim in my capacity as a psychologist at this jail, and I have worked here for four years.' It wasn't until he said those words that I realised how worried I had been about this issue, because of all the crap I had seen on TV. I could see the honesty in his eyes, and a great weight lifted from my shoulders. 'However,' he continued, 'that isn't to say this place isn't dangerous. It is. My best advice for you is what I tell everyone who comes through here, and I tell them because it works.' He had my full attention now. 'Exercise, read, get into a routine,' he was counting off his fingers as he went. 'Eat well, don't stay in your cell as much as you can, keep your mind busy, make use of the programs on offer, don't get into fights, don't piss off the screws and don't do drugs.'

These were ten of the most genuine and useful pieces of advice I have ever received.

CHAPTER 7

Medical

Introduction

The last chapter mentioned the importance of exercising patience. This is especially relevant when dealing with medical services in jail. The jail has a duty of care to you – they want to see you leave the facility on two feet, unscathed. As such, 'front-line' medical care is adequate – if you break your arm or twist your ankle on the oval, you will be seen to quickly and efficiently. However, the same cannot be said for mental health services.

Everyone with ASD is at a different point along the spectrum, so how frustrated you feel about medical services (or lack thereof) will vary. But one thing will be almost certain – the jail will make you jump through multiple hoops before you can even *see* a psychiatrist (which is often who you really need to see because psychologists can't change your medications and the GP will say, 'You have to see the psychiatrist before I can authorise changing your psychoactive medication'). Try to remember this:

1. Excessive worry about medical issues will not speed up the process. On the outside, you could get an appointment

with another doctor, or go to another chemist, but in jail you don't have that luxury. Using the Serenity Prayer (and really believing in it) can be very, very helpful:

Grant me the serenity
To accept the things I cannot change
The courage to change the things I can
And the wisdom to know the difference.

2. Irrespective of your religious views, this adage is true – keep it at the forefront of your mind.
3. Staying patient means you won't be nagging staff. Badgering staff will make them antagonistic towards you and less sympathetic to your plight.

Arriving at the placement jail was the final stop, as I had done my time in the remand and reception jails. I could relax somewhat. This was the last change of environment (jail-wise) I would have to endure. As people with Asperger's know, we like change about as much as a punch to the throat.

Going through the intake process, more relaxed than usual because I knew this would be the last time I would be enduring such measures, I nevertheless remembered to be very clear about my medication when I got to the medical processing part of the intake. When I had been at the remand and reception jails, I had faced the same problem with my meds – namely, instead of ordering the medication when it was running low, they would order it once it had run out. Obviously, they quickly realised they needed to order in advance, so it only affected me for a couple of days at both jails.

However, this placement jail is in a small town about

80 kilometres (50 miles) from the state capital. The other jails had been relatively close to the city, and thus close to the warehouse holding medical stock for prisons. I politely told the head nurse it was important to order this medication before it runs out, not when it runs out. 'Oh yes,' she said with a slight air of indignation. 'Of course. That won't be a problem.'

Of course, it was a problem. I ran out of my medication on Monday and politely asked medical (via a medical slip) to rectify the issue ASAP. No luck for two days, at which point I sent another request form. Still no luck.

By day four without my meds, I was getting frustrated. I wrote a more strongly worded request, which was not rude, did not contain threats or even coarse language. A few hours later I was called to medical. I went down with an air of excitement, thinking, 'Excellent! My meds must be in!' Only, they weren't. They had called me down so the head nurse could berate me for sending more than one request form regarding the issue. 'But it's ongoing,' I said. 'I feel like I have to keep up the pressure or nothing will happen.' I didn't mention I had explained this exact scenario to them upon my arrival – I knew that would only inflame the situation.

'Look,' she said. 'We're doing all we can to get it here, okay?' She smiled. She had a friendly smile.

I relented. 'Okay…but please remember this is important to me.'

'I know.'

She had kind eyes. I believed she really was doing her best to help me. Feeling a bit better, I headed back to my unit. When I got back to the unit, I headed over to the screw's desk to return my prison ID.

'How'd it go?' he enquired.

'Yeah, okay,' I replied. 'They should have it in soon. The nurse was helpful.'

'Good.' He looked at me sideways. 'Because if you had carried on like that, me and a couple of the other COs woulda dragged you into the airlock and belted the fuck out of you for carrying on like a brat.'

'Uh-huh,' I said, shocked. This CO had literally just told me he was planning to beat the shit out of me for requesting access to meds I can't live without. And how is that being a 'brat'? Asking for medication I need?! I still think about that, even these days. It was so strange, and so...unfair. It was almost surreal. It made me feel very, very alone. It was one of the more disconcerting experiences I had while inside.

The anecdote above illustrates why nagging will get you nowhere. The chapter will now break down into two parts:

- physical health
- mental health.

Physical Health

Injuries can be avoided with relative ease. None of the jobs offered to inmates involves particularly dangerous tools or practices, provided you demonstrate the most basic common sense (like not hitting yourself in the face with a hammer). Nor are cells likely to cause injuries through slippage and so on. Provided you follow the lead of more experienced inmates, exercising shouldn't cause injury. Don't overdo it – regular, steady working out is the key to getting bigger – not pushing it to the max every workout session. Injuries from assaults are *relatively* common, but for the most part it's not much more than bruising, swelling and minor cuts and/or abrasions. If the COs witness a fight, you have no choice but to be escorted to medical for a check-up. If the fight is not witnessed by COs, *do not seek help unless something is really wrong, like a broken rib, broken jaw or you're urinating blood, etc.* And even then, lie about how it happened: 'I slipped in the shower, and my jaw smacked against the cistern on the toilet.' Okay, so it's unlikely. But they can't prove it *didn't* happen, and the only way your assailant will get in trouble is if you tell on them – *and you never tell on anybody in jail, ever.* A more detailed discussion of physical confrontation, and how to manage it, can be found later in the book.

If you have a physical medical issue unrelated to a fight:

- Don't wait and see – it's better to be safe than sorry so act in a timely manner.
- Be as specific as you can when filling in medical requests (see Chapter 11 for information on where medical forms are kept).
- If the issue is worsening, alert the COs – they may allow you to go to medical there and then.
- If you are sick and unable to move far, there is the emergency medical intercom in your cell, manned 24 hours a day. The location of these will be obvious.
- Seriously ill or injured prisoners will be treated by para-medics called to the jail.

Remember, no jail wants an inmate to die, so you will be looked after.

Medical issues beyond the scope of the jail

Just like every other citizen, inmates have rights. One of those is the right to basic medical care. If the doctor at the jail is unable to adequately address your physical health needs, he or she can recommend you be put on a transport (or ambulance if time is of the essence) and be taken to a major hospital. Most major cities will have at least one hospital with a secure wing for this very purpose. Inmates may go for a consult or be admitted if necessary. Don't hold any illusions about escaping via this method – this is real life, not Hollywood.

Drug-seeking behaviour

There are doctors and nurses who, for whatever reason, are cynical and dismissive of inmates seeking medication-based treatment. Our draconian drug laws have made some staff view drug addiction as a moral failure rather than a medical issue. Unfortunately, it's nearly impossible for staff to be sure who is chasing the high of drugs versus those who genuinely need them. Jail is enforced sobriety for many inmates, and it's common for them to embrace a life free of drugs. Alternatively, there are those who continue to seek drugs wherever they go, and see jail as an obstacle, not a barrier. There are more of the former – those who see drugs in jail as an expensive and dangerous use of their time. Despite this, staff (including medical staff) are continually on the lookout for anything drug-related – including inmates seeking medications through legitimate channels. This hypervigilance, however well intended, can manifest in denying inmates medications they genuinely need, such as anti-anxiety drugs (like diazepam) or painkillers (like morphine or oxycodone).

Gumball was a mild-mannered guy. He'd been inside going on 15 years. He'd killed an itinerant man while he himself was homeless. He was quiet, and kept mostly to himself. Over the course of a few months he started to experience back pain. A niggle at first, then deteriorating to the point where he was allowed by the screws to stay lying down on his bed during muster (headcount). The screws knew he wasn't bullshitting. He had no history of drug-related behaviour. About four months after his initial request, he was sent to see a specialist at hospital. The specialist said there wasn't a lot he could do, other than minimise movement and keep the area warm. He also wrote Gumball out a script for oxycodone tablets, 5 mg p.r.n. When he arrived back in jail, the doctor looked at the file from the specialist, saw the reference to the oxycodone, and promptly scratched it out with a pen and wrote 'paracetamol' in its place. And the doctor wondered why inmates had it in for him.

If something like this happens to you, the best approach is to gently but relentlessly pursue the issue. It will be frustrating (and at times enraging) but there's no other way to go about it – you're the prisoner, and they're the gatekeepers. At the risk of sounding like a broken record – remember that word: *patience.*

ASD-specific advice
The physical side of medical services doesn't negatively affect those with ASD per se. But it doesn't hurt to be prepared. That is, accept you are part of an underfunded, slow and sometimes indifferent medical system. If a low patience threshold is part of your ASD make-up, it will help to know *prior* to dealing with medical what you may be up against.

Mental Health

Introduction
For the inmate with ASD, how well equipped the jail is to cope with your mental health needs is significant, irrespective of whether they know about your diagnosis (see Chapter 5). As for physical health, it's rarely a significant issue for inmates. People eat meals that meet nutritional requirements, are (almost always)

forbidden to smoke, and drink very little to no alcohol (obviously, any alcohol consumed is brewed illicitly). Non-prescribed drugs are generally avoided, as even socially inept inmates quickly see the danger associated with using illicit drugs in jail. Basically, jail is good for an inmate's physical health.

Sadly, it's not so good for mental health, especially if you are on the spectrum. Whether you have ASD, schizophrenia, depression, anxiety, paranoia, bipolar disorder or attention deficit hyperactivity disorder (ADHD), you will be among your own kind behind bars. Many prisoners have some form of diagnosable mental ailment. Being patient (there's that word again!) and compassionate towards inmates dealing with mental illness is beneficial both to you and your fellow prisoners.

Contrary to the common belief that people with ASD lack empathy, in fact many of them have *high* levels of empathy – exerting sympathy is a quality that comes naturally. Just be careful not to come across as patronising or condescending. A simple 'You okay, mate? You look a bit stressed' is sufficient. It gives the inmate an opportunity to talk if they want, but they can't accuse you of prying. All you did was ask if a visibly distressed inmate wanted to talk. *Never try to stop 'listening' to your empathy – it will help you feel sane and mentally strong.*

The potential vicious cycle
Frustratingly, a healthcare system treating physical injuries with a cavalier approach isn't likely to treat mental ailments any better. Worse, mental health issues are significantly more likely to affect inmates. When people are ignored, and feel their health concerns are treated with callous disregard, frustration levels rise fast. In prison, frustration has ramifications, such as tension, which can lead to aggression between inmates (or inmates and staff), or desperation, which can lead to

self-harming behaviour. Basically, it's in the interest of the jail to keep inmates mentally stable. Sadly most correctional facilities are understaffed and underequipped to deal adequately with mental health problems. Despite this, prisons *do* have a mental health team (or equivalent) and, as an inmate, you have the right to see these people.

Reaching out

Accessing mental health support can seem complicated. A cynic could be forgiven for thinking this is a deliberate ploy to dissuade inmates from making mental health requests. But that's just an opinion, not an assertion. The initial steps are like seeking physical health support:

- Fill in a medical request form, ticking the box for 'mental' or 'psychiatric' help.
- Keep the message regarding details clear and succinct.
- Hand the form to the nurse during AM (morning) medical dispensing. You don't have to be on AM medications to see the nurse – just line up with everyone else.

Remember: if you're experiencing intense, dark thoughts and suspect you may be on the cusp of hurting yourself, tell the nurse or a CO immediately. You will be taken seriously, and jails have special accommodation designed for inmates battling self-harm or suicidal thoughts.

Seeing a psychiatric expert

The process will work something like this:

1. Your medical request will be read by a nurse.
2. The nurse will pass this to the mental health team.

3. An initial assessment will be organised.
4. Depending on the nature of your request, either a psychiatrist *or* a psychologist (or both) will book you in for an appointment.
5. The appointment time/date will be handed to you during med rounds or by a CO. *Either way, you will be informed.*
6. You attend the meeting, where a trained professional will assess you. They may prescribe medications (if they are a psychiatrist) to help with anxiety and stress, such as benzodiazepines (Valium) and/or antipsychotics such as olanzapine (Zyprexa) or quetiapine (Seroquel).

This all seems straightforward on paper, but as with most things in life, the real deal can be slow and frustrating. But don't throw in the towel. If you've come so far, go all the way – in the end, it's in your interest to see it through.

A valuable tip: have your outside doctor send a letter, verifying the medications you were on or have been on in the past. This adds weight to your cause. Doing this requires cooperation from your people on the outside. Make sure at least one person on your phone account is capable of organising things for you in the real world, such as getting a list of your medications and sending it to the jail.

Finally, your time has come
Eventually, you'll find yourself sitting before a psychiatrist. The best thing to do is be totally honest about how you're coping. If you have decided to let them know you have ASD, talk about it. Tell them your fears and worries. You're safe in that room – you can relax. Jail psychiatrists and jail psychologists have seen literally hundreds of inmates, so when they're giving you advice it's likely *good* advice. And they're bound by confidentiality laws, so what's said in there stays in there.

It's helpful to prepare a list of questions for the appointment.
Keep the list succinct and relevant with to-the-point queries. If
there's a medication that you know helps you cope but the jail
took you off it (not an uncommon situation, annoyingly):

- Be polite but firm.
- Listen to their rationale before arguing the point.
- Explain you've been on this medication (or medications)
  before.
- Stress they worked and greatly improved your quality of life.
- If they try to offer an alternative medicine, and you know
  it won't be effective, tell them.
- Be assertive *not* aggressive.

Even in countries where benzodiazepines are considered front-
line treatment for anxiety, psychiatrists who work for correctional
departments are often reluctant to prescribe them. While their
intentions may be noble (stopping drug diverting), sometimes
medication *is* the best method of countering anxiety. If the doctor
is hesitant to use an anti-anxiety medication, try explaining:

- People with ASD frequently rely on benzodiazepines on
  the outside.
- While jails are reluctant to *initiate* benzodiazepine treatment, letters from your doctors can confirm you have been
  a long-term recipient of such medications.
- Anxiety management is an essential for those with ASD.
- Simply *thinking* one may lose access to medications can
  increase anxiety.
- Your new loud, intimidating and violent environment is
  inevitably going to cause anxiety to manifest.
- Cessation of these medications (benzodiazepines) is potentially detrimental to your mental health.

They have a duty of care to you, enshrined in legislation. If the psychiatrist seems reluctant to continue with treatment (even if on the outside it worked wonders), ask them why. Perhaps you can meet each other halfway, and work out a plan that suits both parties.

Life is compromise

This chapter has painted medical services in a black-and-white, you-and-them fashion. To some extent that's a justifiable outlook. However, it's simplistic and doesn't give credit where it's due. Jails have hard-working, compassionate and professional doctors and nurses, hampered by bureaucracy and inadequate funding. Keep this in mind when dealing with medical services. As with *many* facets of jail (and life), it pays to be flexible and willing to compromise. Strive to be a patient patient!

So, they're not playing ball

Sometimes, all the patience and good manners in the world won't guarantee that your mental health needs are met to your satisfaction. If it's a case of metaphorical roadblock after metaphorical roadblock, there are ways to try to circumvent this situation. Try taking one (or all) of the following courses of action:

- Jails *should* have a clear grievance procedure in place. If it is not obvious (like a poster on the wall), ask a CO for a copy.
- Write to the general manager (GM) of the jail – most jails have special envelopes in which you can enclose a letter, which, once sealed, can only be opened by the GM (at least, it's *supposed* to work like this).
- Call/write to an outside party (like a parent, sibling or caregiver) and have them write to the GM on your behalf.

This is effective because if the GM knows you are telling the outside world about lacklustre services, they have an incentive to shut you up, which will mean medication, not horrible treatment – they know people are watching.

- Contact the head of prison medical services for the whole state. You will need third-party help for this, as medical will be reluctant to divulge who's in charge at the very top.
- Contact the medical ombudsman. A list of official numbers will be near the phones. Failing that, ask a CO for the number.

Unfortunately, going through this arduous process doesn't guarantee a positive outcome. If, after all this, medications are *still* not forthcoming, ask to see a psychologist about dealing with stress in non-medicinal ways, such as mindfulness and cognitive-behavioural therapy (CBT). Chapter 17 will explore this in greater detail.

Remember – play it cool. It's frustrating not having your mental health ailments treated seriously, but try to *always keep your cool*. Throwing a chair at the doctor or punching a hole in the wall of their office isn't conducive to your cause. Sometimes, it will feel like they are treating you like a number or, worse, an irritation. *Don't let them win* – if you flip out and assault a staff member, not only will you suffer the consequences, but you're *less* likely to have your medical needs met. People with ASD are resilient, tough and tenacious – embrace this when you feel frustrated and helpless. Your inner strength is far, far greater than you think.

Finally
Resorting to extreme measures to convince the authorities of your desperation may backfire. While self-mutilation and antisocial behaviour might make you *feel* like you're in control,

nothing could be further from the truth. Such actions can result in you being placed on an involuntary treatment order (ITO) or other similarly named protection model. This will affect where you are housed in the jail, what programs you can access, who you can interact with and even your chances of an early release. If they think you are a threat to yourself, or others, you may find yourself being 'released' into a psychiatric facility, rather than home. And that may be *worse* than jail.

I was once sent back to the placement jail for a parole violation. I didn't like my parole officer and would often go into our fortnightly meetings wasted – but on methadone and oxazepam, both prescribed by a doctor – so she couldn't pin anything on me.

In hindsight, being a provocative little shit probably wasn't the best idea, because she ended up getting me a good one in the end. She rang me at about 3.45 pm on a Friday afternoon, asking that I come in for a meeting. I knew we had one scheduled for the following Tuesday, so I was somewhat surprised. Also, I was in the city, at least an hour and a half away by public transport. I told her this, but promised I would do my best to get there anyway. Obviously, I didn't make it, but I didn't stress on it – I figured I was seeing her on Tuesday anyway so there was no big deal.

When I went to my Tuesday meeting, I had only been in her office for five minutes when there was a knock on the door. She asked if I could open it. I knew at that point I was fucked. I opened it to see two burly, sour-faced coppers, handcuffs at the ready. I didn't even try to protest. They slapped the cuffs on and off I went, for a '28-day sanction'.

A 28-day sanction is never really 28 days. All it means

is that they (the authorities) have 28 days to write to you in jail, explaining that you are in jail and why. My reason was 'Failure to attend a pre-arranged meeting'.

The reason this little jail-tale is included in the chapter on medical is because, as mentioned, I had been on methadone and oxazepam, both prescribed by my psychiatrist. I needed them to feel normal. I needed them to endure socialising (socialising being one of my least favourite things to do, as other people with Asperger's would understand).

I knew I wouldn't be able to get methadone in jail, but a benzo like Valium was plausible. To cut a long story short, I began the process of trying to get on to Valium in the second week of my incarceration.

Four months and two weeks later, I saw the prison psychiatrist, who promptly put me on 15 mg per day, agreeing I needed it and it was in my best interest to have it. Four days later, my parole came through. At least it had given me some focus, I suppose.

CHAPTER 8

A Normal Day in Prison

Introduction

This chapter is a basic explanation of what to expect day to day. Routine is the cornerstone of keeping boredom at bay and making the days go faster, so the sooner you establish one the better. For those with ASD, knowing in advance how the unit runs will help you pre-plan activities like exercise and downtime.

Please note
Different jails will have different procedures. These differences will be slight, and generally apply to the following:

- What time cells are opened (am).
- What time you are 'locked down' (pm).
- Lunchtime.
- Dinnertime.
- Medications times (both am and pm).

- What times (and for how long) cell access is during the day.
- What day/time your unit has oval/gym access.
- Visits.

All maximum security jails share similar protocol. You won't move from remand jail to placement jail and discover a completely different, inverted and confusing new regime to deal with. Differences will be small and easy to assimilate, which is a bonus for those with ASD.

The Daily Breakdown: Unlock

The cells will be opened at approximately 7.30 am. Cells are opened one of two ways, depending on the jail's age and what the standard operating procedure (SOP) is:

1. An old-fashioned walk-around, where two COs come along and manually unlock the door with a key. If they do this, ensure your unit is clean. Also, *if* you have any contraband lying around, clean it up nice and early!
2. The more modern 'popping' of doors – they open automatically, either simultaneously (not as likely) or one after the other in relatively rapid succession (more likely). If the SOP is 'popping', *ensure your gear for the day (pens, noodles, writing paper, playing cards, etc.) is ready to go, and outside your cell before shutting the door.* The COs can and do refuse to open doors after they have been shut. It's done to remind you who's in charge. If an important document is in your cell, and you need it but had no way of knowing in advance (like an unexpected visit from the

parole officer) a polite request to the COs will likely be met with compliance. But if you left your pen/book/chocolate in there, you'll be waiting until access to get it.

Often a unit will use one technique or the other, in a random fashion. One can assume this is for security purposes.

Remember – unless you are visibly unwell, you are required to exit your cell during morning unlock. The authorities need to know precisely how many inmates are inside the jail perimeter, because people come and go for various reasons (as discussed in Chapter 4). They don't need some idiot amusing themselves by hiding in their cell during headcount, sending the jail into a frenzy trying to establish no one has escaped. One could be forgiven for assuming the COs could just unlock the cell door to confirm/deny the presence of the 'missing' inmate, but at first they don't know for certain *who* is missing. The following anecdote is based on an allegedly true story, heard from a reliable source.

Jails regularly go into lockdown all of a sudden for one reason or another – sometimes there's an issue in another unit, like a serious medical issue for which an ambulance has been called, or a high-profile inmate is coming in to the jail, or even if there are storm clouds right over the jail and the GM doesn't want a prisoner getting zapped.

Over the course of my incarceration, I lost track of the number of times we were required to be locked down. One lockdown I remember clearly, because I got the details from a long-term prisoner down at medical a couple of days later. Apparently, some inmate had decided to hide in his cell during muster, and it had thrown the numbers out. Two hours later they found him. They took him to the DU (detention unit) where he stayed a week in solitary. Then, when he got back to his unit, he was promptly given a bashing (nothing too serious) for causing all the boys (I'm talking over 1000 guys in dozens of units across the whole jail) to have to sit in their cells twiddling their thumbs while he played hide-and-seek for his own amusement.

Breakfast (7.00–9.00 am)

After unlock, most inmates make a beeline for the boiler to make their coffee or tea. For those with ASD, it's easier to let the caffeine-hungry throng settle down before making your morning beverage. You don't want to bump into someone grumpy and sleep-deprived, spill their own coffee on them and have to deal with the fallout. It's much easier just to wait a few minutes. After people have got their caffeine fix (and nicotine fix outside in the yard if the jail allows smoking), people start on breakfast. If the unit has a toaster, get into the habit of procuring a couple (a couple – no need for greed) of pieces of bread from dinner the night before and keeping it in your cell overnight. You will have to wait until you can get your hands on an empty bread bag to do this, but don't worry, they're plentiful and this shouldn't be difficult. Then you have fresh bread for toast in the morning. Margarine and other spreads will generally be kept at your designated table. For information about 'designated tables', see Chapter 14.

Your communal food box (which is kept under or near your designated table) *should* have cereal in it. If it doesn't, find out when cereal arrives, and try to make sure your table gets its share.

If you miss out on a decent breakfast for the first few days, don't stress – lunch and dinner is always evenly distributed, and you will quickly work out the best way to get some food into your belly in the morning, even if it means buying some cereal and long-life milk on buy-up and eating it prior to unlock.

AM Medication (Approximately 8.00 am)

Morning medications will be called about 45 minutes after unlock. Distribution is straightforward: get a cup of water (your own cup), line up and patiently wait for your turn to see the nurse, who will confirm your identity with the CO, then give you your medications. After swallowing your meds, your mouth is looked in briefly by a CO. This is a quick visual inspection – by no means invasive. There are three very important things to keep in mind regarding medication:

1. If you like to go into the yard first thing after unlock, *don't* miss the call for medication. COs *don't* want to chase your medication around because you were busy staring out the fence and not paying attention.
2. Don't tell other inmates what you are taking. Inmates look to 'newbies' in the hope that benzodiazepines (and other valuable medications) are prescribed to you. Use your body to block other inmates in the line from *seeing* what you are being given – these guys know what the pill(s) they want look like, even from 2 metres away.
3. *Do not* try to 'divert' your meds (hold in your mouth to retrieve later). If caught, the penalty is quite sharp (a week in solitary). It can also affect other prisoners. For example, they may start conducting more thorough checks during medication time – and this will be blamed on you. If you're serious about minimising stress, avoid diverting altogether.

For more information on 'diverting', see Chapter 9.

First Access (9.00–10.30 am)

At around 9.00 am the COs will call out 'Cell access!' You can choose to go back into your cell or stay out to exercise, play cards, socialise and so on. For more suggestions on how to pass the time, see Chapter 10. To access your cell, stand close to your door after they make the announcement.

> **Please note**
> Having your cell door opened during access periods doesn't mean you have to go in. Inmates stand by their doors so they can retrieve or put back an item of property. Shut the door once you have retrieved your items – the COs want doors open or shut, not ajar for 15 minutes.

Headcount (10.30 am)

Cells are unlocked at 10.30 am (approximately) and, like it or not, you need to come out for the first of two headcounts conducted daily. Two headcounts a day is the goal – often there's a discrepancy in the numbers and they need to do a recount – and if the *second* count is out, the whole prison goes into lockdown until the COs figure out what's happening. The headcount process varies from prison to prison, but it is usually done one of two ways:

1. Everybody stands by their cell door, and the COs come around checking your ID card against your face.

2. All inmates assemble in the yard, usually in a line around the wall, in order according to cell number. A CO will then call out last names, and as yours is called you step away from the wall and walk into the unit.

Headcount is simple and almost impossible to mess up. Having said that, remember the word *almost*.

. . . .

During a stint in one of the rougher units, we were doing morning muster and the TV was on, the communal TV. It hadn't seemed particularly loud until we all stopped playing cards and laughing and carrying on.

'Right,' says the screw. 'Somebody turn that TV off.' Nobody moves. 'Okay,' she says, 'if someone doesn't switch off that TV, I'll have you all locked down for the rest of the day.' Still, no one moves.

She had backed herself into a corner – by demanding somebody essentially 'volunteer' to turn off the TV, she's asking them to paint a big red target on their back.

Eventually another screw showed some common sense and just turned it off themselves, with a warning that next muster the TV must be off.

Regarding a scenario like this – never comply with the request. Even if directly asked, say in a firm voice, 'Chief, if you want it turned down, do it yourself.' This may go against your natural instincts, the words may feel foreign coming from your mouth, but *you must never appear to be on the side of the COs*.

This is only applicable to 'public' interactions with staff. If a CO asks you to clean your cell because it isn't up to scratch, then you do it. It sounds somewhat confusing, especially for those with ASD, but you will pick up the nuances quicker than you think. Basically, if other inmates are watching, you want to be Mr Uncooperative with COs. If it's just you, and a CO is asking you to make your bed, you cooperate.

Lunch (12.00–1.00 pm)

You will be required to stay out of your cell once morning headcount is finished, as the COs don't want to have to do another unlock when lunch arrives. If you have special dietary needs (and you have told the relevant people), your lunch will be marked with your name on it. The kitchen worker will call out to you, so pay attention. Condiments should be in your table's communal box.

People don't go hungry in prison unless they choose to, such as during a hunger strike. Don't worry about food – if push comes to shove, a more senior member of the inmates will ensure you get a meal. Lots of inmates detest bullying, and make it clear by gestures such as making sure that even the most timid, nervous inmate gets their food.

> **Please note**
> If you have lunchtime meds, the nurse will know about it and make a visit to your unit, and the COs will call out your name or come and find you.

Second Access (1.00–2.30 pm)

After lunch the COs will again call out 'Cell access!' You'll notice more inmates taking advantage of this access for a post-lunch nap. For someone with ASD, an afternoon nap may interfere with getting a good night's sleep. Of course, this doesn't apply to everyone on the spectrum, but keep it in mind.

Second Headcount (2.30 pm)

About 90 minutes to two hours after the second access, you have to vacate your cells for the remainder of the afternoon. A second headcount will be conducted at about 2.30 pm.

PM Medications (Approximately 4.00 pm)

Remember – the onus is on you to be aware and listening for the medicine call. PM medications are harder to miss, as more inmates are medicated in the evening and a longer line forms.

Please note
Not all medications are dispensed via the trolleys that visit each unit. Some medications are deemed too 'high risk' to be dispensed outside the medical wing, such as:

- powerful pain medications like morphine, oxycodone or hydrocodone
- steroid medications
- insulin.

Inmates on these medications will be told by a CO what time to visit the medical wing, and the time won't change (and if it *does*, you will be clearly told about it). It's usually around 4.00 pm. It will become routine – you politely ask a CO for your ID card, and if they don't already know, explain why you need it. If they're sceptical, they can ring medical and verify the situation.

Dinner (4.30 pm)

After PM medications, dinner arrives. Depending on the jail, it will be served one of two ways:

1. Individual servings in packaging.
2. Served by other inmates onto your plate from heated food trays.

Both systems have their merits and problems. The individually packed method is effective in making sure nobody misses out, but servings are not particularly large. Being served by other inmates is good because, generally, you get a bigger meal. On the other hand, *because* it's being served by inmates, it adds a social element to the process, something that the inmate with ASD would rather avoid. However, from an anecdotal perspective, getting an adequate amount of food *won't* be jeopardised because an inmate has ASD.

Lockdown (5.00 pm)

Around 4.55 pm, a CO will call out 'Lockaway!' As with morning unlock, it will either be a walk-around manual unlock, or the electronic 'popping' of the doors. You will have about five to ten minutes to gather up your stuff and be ready to go into your cell. During this time:

- Clean your designated table – COs can (and sometimes do) throw out items not in the table's communal box.
- Gather any food you want to bring into your cell and put it near your door.
- Have all your 'day things' (exercise equipment, notebook, pen, noodles and so on) near your cell door. Prison etiquette protects it during the day, but it needs to come into your cell at night.
- Remember your washing if it was a wash day. (For more on washing, see Chapter 11.)

Lockdown is usually quick and efficient – the COs want to go home, and most prisoners look forward to some downtime in their cells.

Night Time

At night, COs will come around every two hours or so and briefly shine a torch through the window in your door. They do this to:

1. check you are still there
2. check you are not dead
3. check you appear physically okay.

This happens about four times a night, and there's nothing that can be done about it. Putting up something to block the COs torches won't work: they will tell you to take it down, and non-compliance means they take it down by force. This will be loud and annoy the whole unit – something you don't want to have to explain come the morning. It isn't like the COs are trying to be obnoxious – it's their job. Jail suicide happens, and it's important that jails treat the issue seriously. Besides, after a few weeks you won't even notice them.

....

Irrespective of how a day had gone for me behind bars – be it boring, hectic, interesting, surprising (but usually boring), I always looked forward to lockdown at the end of the day, especially if I had 'achieved' that day. My definition of 'achieving' was doing my cardio exercise, my calisthenic muscle-building and getting through the day without excessive negative thinking. But it was more than that – getting locked down meant 14 hours of solitude. Fourteen hours of blissful, blissful peace and quiet. Jail echoes a lot, and there are almost no soft things to sit or rest on during the day, so as an Aspie with sensory sensitivities, a clean soft bed and no sudden, loud sounds was heavenly.

There's a widely held misconception that people in jail are always suffering, in some way or another, but it's not true. Some of my best, most peaceful memories are from jail. Some of my biggest belly laughs – you know, the one where you literally double over because you can't laugh any harder – occurred while in jail. Some of the most kind and brave acts of selflessness I have seen were during my time inside.

I would mull over these things while I was lying in my cell, warm, with a belly full of food, and think, 'Yeah, life could be a lot worse...'

CHAPTER 9

Drugs in Jail

Introduction

Humans have always used psychoactive drugs to ease pain, help them feel more relaxed or give them energy, and it's no different in jail. At least, it's no different in the sense that inmates are humans, and some of them will seek drugs behind bars, even if the cost is substantially higher than on the outside. Taking drugs in jail is problematic for those inmates who choose to use. COs know what's going on (in a general sense) and can spring a urine test (UT) on a suspected drug user anytime. But worse, getting caught up in the drug scene can cause tension and even violence between inmates. Many friendships are soured because of drug use.

ASD, Drugs and Jail

ASD causes anxiety, exacerbates sensory sensitivities and creates a dislike of hypersocial environments. Hence, drugs may seem like an appealing and effective 'quick fix'. But that 'quick fix' comes at a price, and not just a financial one. For starters, procuring illicit substances means having to deal with people who are in it for themselves – not to help you. The drug scene in jail is fraught with violence, paranoia and desperation. If anxiety, depression or chronic pain is affecting you, address the problem legitimately. The process may be arduous, and at times frustrating, but the outcome will be worth it – prescribed anti-anxiety or painkilling medication. The process of obtaining these medications legitimately is explained in the mental health section of Chapter 7.

Drugs in Jail – The Basics

There are two subgroups of drugs in jail:

1. Drugs that have been brought *into* the jail in a clandestine manner. These drugs may be pharmaceutical (such as buprenorphine) or they may be 'street' drugs (such as heroin or marijuana).
2. Pharmaceuticals that have been 'diverted' during medication time. These are drugs like quetiapine, diazepam and pregabalin.

The first group causes more problems, as they are more valuable. This is because (a) they're more potent, and (b) getting them into jail is difficult.

It's a jail – how do illegal drugs even get in there? Someone once said 'necessity is the mother of invention', and it's this philosophy that drives inmates to take creative measures to ensure they get their prized 'hit'. Hundreds of inmates, all after the same thing, become amazingly innovative, especially when they have ample time to think about it. Without revealing any specific methods, drugs generally come into jail in the following ways:

- via visits
- through the mail
- swallowed
- in the anal (or vaginal) cavity.

The authorities try to stem the flow of illicit drugs into jails, but for every stash they uncover, there are ten that get through. Because cavity searches are mostly illegal in developed countries, the COs can't stop inmates utilising this primitive but effective method of bringing drugs in via the body.

Different Jails, Different Drugs

In Chapter 3, the three categories of incarceration – remand, reception and placement – are explained. Most countries follow a similar format – that is, a system where inmates move through different facilities as they progress through different stages of the judicial process. Different facilities have different drug dynamics. For example, remand jails (or any jail that inmates come to from the watch house) have more drugs, both in terms of quantity and variety. This is because many inmates are either recidivist offenders or are in jail on a parole breach. They knew their return to prison was a matter of when, not if. They also knew to come in 'prepared' – they will have had a package of drugs, often along with cut-down needles, tightly wrapped for insertion into a body cavity. They would carry it on them at all times, so when the police come knocking, they would quickly 'shaft' the package (insert it into the anus or vagina). Drugs brought in using this method only last so long, so as inmates progress through the system, drugs must come in via other means.

Visits at reception jails are rare, because inmates come and go quickly, and security clearance for visits can take weeks. Because of this, reception jails have fewer 'street' drugs inside. Having said this, reception jails are not drug-free – there's just less drug activity. Placement jails are often situated far from city centres. This influences the number of visits, which in turn affects the quantity of drugs coming in.

Why Do Some Inmates Do Drugs?

The primary answer to this question is the same as it is on the outside – some people feel they need help coping with life. But in jail, it's more than just that. There are other factors that can motivate an inmate to use:

- Boredom – organising, negotiating and attaining drugs gives inmates a sense of purpose.
- Status – just like on the outside, inmates will vie for the position of dominance in the drug trade.
- Getting one over the COs – inmates enjoy the subterfuge andthe adrenaline surge they get from breaking the rules.
- Friendship – drugs allow people to bond over a common interest.

Drugs Coming into Jail from Outside

It is a bad idea to become involved in taking drugs that are coming into jail illegally, for several reasons.

Financially

The price of smuggled drugs is very steep. Here's an example (without divulging the specific drug):

- Eight milligrams of this substance on the street = $35 to $50.
- Eight milligrams of the same substance in jail = $400 to $600.

Obviously, inmates can't waltz up to an ATM and withdraw cash, so drugs are paid for in one of several ways:

- Sellers will expect the customer to buy them $X amount worth of buy-up.
- Customers talk in code to their people on the outside, who arrange payment to the seller's people.
- Sellers ask the buyer to do 'favours' for them, such as assaulting another inmate.
- Rare, but also used, is the trading of drugs for sexual favours.

For most inmates, the massive increase in cost is incentive enough to avoid consuming drugs. If money isn't an issue, there are other reasons to avoid using while inside.

Mentally

Anecdotally, inmates doing drugs originating from the outside seem to endure higher levels of stress. They worry about where their next 'fix' is coming from, whether they have enough to pay for it, whether someone will come along with a better offer (outbid them), and so on. Unless under the influence, most users inside are *not* happy people – even the most affluent and influential inmates end up detoxing from time to time.

Keep things predictable and stable – two qualities people

with ASD thrive on. Choosing to immerse yourself in the drug world is not the least bit conducive to minimising stress and potential conflict.

Personal safety

If you do drugs that have come into the jail from outside:

- You run the risk of being randomly searched by COs. If they find drugs/drug equipment, not only will you spend a few days/nights in solitary confinement, but other inmates will worry you might 'give them up', especially if you're a relatively new inmate.
- You could be 'stood over' for it (forced to hand it over). And if those drugs belonged to someone else, that inmate won't care you were stood over – they're only interested in getting their drugs or money, or, failing that, retribution (on you).
- Very few prisons provide clean needles for injection, so intravenous (IV) users run an elevated risk of catching Hepatitis C or HIV.
- Inmates can substitute the actual drug with another compound, so they get the high and you take an unknown compound.

There is little to be gained from involving yourself in the drug scene. This is especially applicable for people with ASD, as social naivety can be exploited. Inmates will respect you if you say no and mean it. Mean it in your eyes. If you're there because drugs, in some way, contributed to your offending, say, 'I came here to get *off* the shit. It got me in here. I'm not letting it control me again.' Addicts respect this, and there will be others in the unit who feel the same way you do.

Please note
Even if you have made the choice not to use inside, *you must respect the choice of others to use*. You won't make any friends by lecturing people on the evils of drugs. Live and let live.

I was out in the yard exercising one day – nothing particularly unusual or interesting about that – except on this occasion I happened to be standing near the 'drug corner' (the part of the yard that can be visually obscured by inmates, so the screws can't see what's happening), and there was a bunch of inmates busy mixing up shots for themselves. Out of curiosity I watched them, but subtly. I knew they wouldn't notice. Addicts are transfixed when mixing up their drugs.

One guy put the communal needle in the spoon, sucked back his hit, and got a friend to inject him because the needle was so blunted he needed help from a more experienced user. He has his shot, pulls out the needle, and hands it to his mate. Then, without even rinsing the needle, his mate sticks it straight back into the same spoon, pulls back his hit, rubs some margarine onto his injection site to help with lubrication, and rams the needle straight in there. I could hear the popping sound as it punctured his skin.

I include this anecdote only to illustrate how far some people will go to escape to a nicer place (in their heads). I understand that. I was an intravenous drug user for ten years. If it could be injected, in it would go. But in jail I found the strength to say no, and that was a major turning point for me. It is for others too. If you're in a similar boat, use your time behind bars to get healthy and clean. It might save your life.

The Second Type of Drug Usage – Drug Diverting

The other type of illicit drug consumption in jail comes from inmates 'diverting' their medications and selling/swapping them to other inmates.

What is 'diverting'?

Diverting medication is the practice of appearing to swallow medication when in fact the person has pushed the tablet into the corner of their mouth, for quick retrieval in the minute or two after they are dosed.

If a CO is checking people's mouths, isn't this a risky practice? Absolutely. Inmates are often caught diverting; the punishment is a 'breach' and usually a brief stay (less than one week) in the DU. 'Breaches' and the 'DU' will be explained in Chapter 11.

However, it's other inmates, rather than the prison authorities, who you should be worried about if you get caught diverting medication. If you're new to jail, or even if you're in a new unit, and haven't had time to prove you're trustworthy, it can get messy. If you're caught diverting, other inmates will worry that you could end up telling the COs things best kept quiet. Most inmates caught diverting won't be divulging any information, but if you're new, and inmates can 'sense' you're different (ASD), then there could be trouble.

Avoid diverting altogether. Besides, depriving yourself of Valium or Seroquel will upset your mental equilibrium.

Drugs in demand

Medications other inmates might want:

- benzodiazepines (like Valium)
- antipsychotics (like Seroquel)

- drugs for neuropathic pain (like Lyrica)
- weak opiate-based painkillers (like Tramadol)
- tricyclic antidepressants (like Endep).

These are medications that have prison value. If you are on any of these medications (especially benzodiazepines or strong painkillers), *keep it to yourself.* Of course, you can't control other inmates, so if an inmate starts grilling you over your meds, remember:

1. If asked if you are on anything 'good', lie. Say you are on a heartburn tablet and Prozac, or some other medications that are of no value.
2. As mentioned in Chapter 8, when you get to the front of the line, use your body to obstruct the view of other inmates, so they can't see what meds you are being given.
3. Don't show any interest in what other inmates are on. Act like meds are a hassle. This will make it look like you aren't on anything 'fun', which is exactly what you want the med line vultures to think.

Once, in reception jail, I dropped one of my pills. It bounced and rolled along the floor. The inmate behind me, an annoying brat, picked it up and gave it to me, as there were other people watching, including a screw. Annoyingly, the tablet happened to be diazepam (Valium). The jail was in the process of weaning me off benzos, so they were becoming increasingly valuable to me.

When I dropped this Valium pill, I was three days from stopping the medication. I knew the brat knew it was Valium, so I pre-empted him by telling him later, in the yard, that the pills were going to stop in a couple of days. He didn't believe me but I stood my ground and said, 'Look around you...nobody's on Valium here. Why would I be any different?'

It kept him off my back, but for the next two weeks, up until I got my transfer to placement jail, he would make sure he was behind me in the med line, watching like a hawk to see if I really had been taken off the pills.

Taking Other People's Diverted Medications

The stakes are much higher trying to get drugs *into* the prison rather than diverting, so trade in diverted medications is less intense. Regardless, the same 'rules' still apply – for example, if you get diverted meds on credit, you can get hurt if you don't pay up on time and so on. But forget about all the jailhouse stuff for a moment and ask yourself: is my brain, knowing I have ASD, worth messing around with? Especially in an environment like jail? You need to be at your best, your sharpest, and that won't happen if you mess around with other inmates' medications.

A Final Note on Drug Use Inside

Prison is difficult enough for people with ASD. Fooling around with medications that weren't prescribed to you or choosing to immerse yourself in the sordid world of using street drugs inside will put you at a distinct disadvantage. This book is written as a guide to help those with ASD cope with the jail system, and that is complicated enough. Adding illicit drugs to the mix will only serve to exacerbate this complexity, not diminish it. Jail and drugs – it just doesn't work.

Years before I went to prison, I read this guy's account of his time in jail. The piece of writing was in a now-defunct publication written by, and for, drug users. It espoused a harm minimisation approach. It's a shame it's no longer in circulation. The author talked about how most of the fights, bashings and intimidation stemmed, in one way or another, from drug use.

When I read his story, I never expected to wind up behind bars myself, but his writing had a strong effect on me. The message was very clear: if you want to avoid trouble while in jail, avoid drugs.

Looking back, I'm extremely grateful it left such an impression on me, as when I found myself locked up, and very stressed, I knew nothing could really justify using. So, I didn't, and it was during my stints behind bars that I was able to get clean for the first time in years, and just knowing I could be clean, and able to function, was a watershed moment in my journey of recovery.

For me, jail was enforced rehab – and I'll be forever grateful for that. Thinking about it now, it may well have been jail that ultimately allowed me to break free from the shackles of addiction.

CHAPTER 10

Keeping Busy

Introduction

When released from jail, the most common question you will hear is: 'So, what's jail like?!' There are many answers to this: intimidating, interesting, unique, harsh, lonesome, difficult, humorous... The list goes on. However, one word will describe much of your experience: boring. It may seem odd, as most people fear jail, but it's true – a lot of the time, jail is just...boring.

Why Boredom Can Be Worse for People with ASD

People with ASD usually thrive on mental stimulation, often derived from their 'special interest' (SI). An SI serves many purposes, not just mental stimulation:

- relaxation
- an effective thought-blocker
- an emotion regulator

- calms and soothes
- provides purpose and a sense of achievement
- gives energy
- takes you away from reality
- helps put things into perspective.

Jail takes a lot from you, the most prominent loss being that of your freedom. It can also take away your ability to engage with your SI. Losing your ability to enjoy activities that provide pleasurable feelings, thoughts and emotions can be difficult to deal with. *Don't despair!* It's a matter of perspective; nobody is asking you to stop *thinking* about your SI, nor will you be denied the ability to re-engage with it upon release. Try applying the Serenity Prayer mentioned in Chapter 7. You *can't* change your incarceration. You *can't* change the fact you are unable to engage with your SI as much as you would like. You *can* change how this affects you. The best way to avoid ruminating is to keep busy, because (a) you will think less about what you don't have, and (b) developing a strong routine is essential for good mental health. There's already structure and routine in place, as discussed in Chapter 8. But having predictable unlock, medication and meal times is not enough structure to ensure you go to sleep at night tired and content. You will need to put in some work to facilitate this.

The Devil Makes Work for Idle Hands

As discussed in Chapter 9, using while inside will most likely end badly. The same applies for any sort of cloak-and-dagger activities where the goal is to try to get one over the COs. Use time constructively – it will serve three main purposes:

1. Minimising anxiety.
2. The time will go faster when you are happy and busy.
3. COs are constantly making notes regarding the behaviour of all inmates. When you are going to sentencing, or have been sentenced and are applying for parole, notes that paint a positive picture are *exactly* what you want.

Please note
While there is more to do behind bars than one might think, activities organised by the jail will differ from facility to facility.

Social vs Solo Activities

Keeping busy is easier than you might think. Of course, a spanner is thrown into the works when you add the dynamic of ASD.

Some inmates latch on to one another like attracting magnets, and become genuinely good friends. You will see these types (usually between two and five inmates), and they seem almost dependent on each other: they eat together, exercise together, play cards together, cut laps in the yard together, etc. It seems they're in each other's company from unlock to lock-in. Inmates with ASD would find this exhausting, nerve-wracking and suffocating.

That's the extreme end of a spectrum. At the other end is the loner – the inmate who keeps to himself, keeps conversation at meal times to a minimum, and chooses to stay in at access times. They're minimising social exposure. These 'loners' aren't necessarily on the autism spectrum (although some would be), but are inmates who simply prefer their own company.

How much a person socialises isn't indicative of happiness – there are inmates who hypersocialise *because* they are, in fact, quite unhappy. There are other reasons inmates may 'hypersocialise', such as:

- To form a sense of identity (through 'collective' identity).
- For safety (this is more applicable in jails with a stronger 'gang culture' and/or racial tensions, such as correctional facilities in the US).
- To create a 'surrogate' family – especially if actual family support is minimal or non-existent.
- Drug use – inmates involved in the drug scene often want to spend as much time with their cohorts as possible, lest they 'miss out'.
- They had pre-existing friendships, either established in jail or prior to incarceration.

Doing it Solo

Having ASD doesn't mean you will want to completely isolate yourself. It also *doesn't* mean you won't find a group of people who are the right fit for you. If you choose to do it solo, remember: it's one thing to be a lone wolf, quite another to be the surly and rude loner. For inmates with ASD, minimising social interaction will, by default, decrease the risk of making a social 'mistake' and having to deal with the consequences. But don't cut off your nose to spite your face – turning down friendships to avoid *theoretical* exchanges is perhaps too cautious. Most inmates with ASD have friends inside, usually other inmates who are slight 'misfits', or inmates who are more intellectually inclined. Inmates with ASD can also form strong friendships with neurotypical, seasoned prisoners, provided they 'click'. It's more common than you may think. Humans are 'attracted' (in a non-sexual sense) to an eclectic mix of people throughout life, and it's like that in jail too.

While doing a small stint for breaching parole in placement jail, I found some other inmates, well, difficult. This was the jail unit where they thought it the pinnacle of hilarity to watch my reflex action to being poked. However, I had a small group of friends who I talked to about lightweight topics, like girls and cars and movies and so on. None of these guys seemed to be on the spectrum, nor did they pick me as being socially 'different'.

Anyway, one day a new inmate came in (nothing abnormal about that) and you could tell he was a seasoned prisoner, or 'old head', as the saying goes. He was big, strong and Aboriginal (which in Australian jails is an advantage, as they are, sadly, overrepresented in the judicial system, and as such are not strangers to correctional facilities). I assumed he would gravitate towards the other Aboriginals (although there was no racial tension in the jail), but he didn't. He ended up sitting and hanging out with me and my small group of friends.

At first, I wondered why, but it became apparent quite quickly why he was attracted to our group – he was very intelligent and, moreover, was not interested in the same old jail talk about how many guns an inmate used to have, how many fights they've won (no one ever talks about the fights they lost), how many Ferraris they used to own, how many supermodels they've slept with – you get the picture. It gets tedious quickly, and it seemed by that stage he too was over it, as he seemed far more interested in not talking about crime and not gossiping about other inmates, but rather talking about normal things.

I include this anecdote to illustrate (a) don't judge a book by its cover, and (b) you never know who you will end up friends with. While at first you may feel lonely and unsure of how to fill your day, things can come along and surprise you, and make your journey that little bit more comfortable.

Don't Try to Sleep Away Your Sentence

Keeping busy is important for sleep. But because there is a limited amount of activities for inmates to engage in, it's common for inmates to go in to their cells during access and sleep. This method works for some, especially if they take sedatives during PM medications. But if you have trouble falling asleep naturally (as is common in ASD), I strongly recommend that you *don't* sleep during access time. It can leave you feeling warped and interfere with night sleep – and being stuck in a 3 × 3-metre cell at night, unable to sleep, is very frustrating. Try to save cell time for:

- sleeping (at night!)
- unwinding at the end of the day
- taking a break from socialising during the day
- metaphorically recharging your batteries.

Keeping Active During the Day

In most jails, you have 14 mandatory hours in your cell (5.00 pm lockaway to 7.00 am unlock). Fourteen hours may seem like a long time to fill, especially without access to your SI, but humans are resourceful and, once you establish routine, the rest falls into place. Activities you can engage in break down into four main areas:

1. social activities
2. jail-based educational courses and group activities
3. solo activities
4. work (either in-unit work or 'outside' work – industries, the kitchen, industrial laundry, etc.) (see Chapter 11, for more detail).

Social Activities

Cards

Playing cards is a good way to pass the time and 'socialise'. It's the most common group activity for inmates, and it does effectively help pass the time. With the game being front and centre, socialising is lightweight. It's the opposite of having a one-on-one conversation. When socialising is the by-product, and not the focus of an activity, it suits inmates with ASD. The games are not difficult to pick up, and can be quite fun. However, try to remember the following:

- Don't be a sore loser or obnoxious winner.
- Don't 'invite' yourself into a game – wait to be asked or, if you have been in the unit long enough to have made some friends, start up your own game.
- *Do not*, I repeat, *do not* gamble. Seasoned inmates can make it look like you and your partner lost the game, when in fact your 'partner' was in on it, and it's *you* who really lost.

Other games

Aside from cards (bought from the buy-up list – see Chapter 11), there are chess boards, Uno, Scrabble, Monopoly, backgammon, Trivial Pursuit, etc. Remember: inmates like to be able to play chess/Scrabble/backgammon, etc. with all the pieces, so abide by the golden rule and be sure to keep everything together and tidy when you return games to the designated shelf/room/cupboard.

Group exercising

Group workouts tend to involve four people or fewer – too many people can equal a long time spent on any one piece of equipment, which is inconsiderate to fellow inmates.

Why exercise in a group? The theory is that if you have peer pressure to motivate you, collectively you can all become fit and healthy. Unfortunately, it can work the other way too: when one person expresses reluctance, then someone else does and before you know it you're playing cards. People with ASD generally fare better working out alone. Not because working out in a group is inferior, but rather if you learn to train alone, you rely only upon yourself. Keeping fit is something you must *want*, not something you feel you *should* do. Nobody ever gets teased for working out alone. In fact, if you show devotion – and get out there come rain, hail or shine, it will earn you respect (and a strong body).

And it doesn't matter if you're not experienced at working out; simply observe the other inmates – especially the bigger guys. Watch and learn techniques and use them in your own exercise regime. Nobody will mind if you mimic an exercise technique. Inmates interested in fitness are happy to share techniques and advice with others. Just don't ask them questions when they are in the middle of their workout – approach them later, and explain you want to maximise results. Make it obvious you aren't looking to work out *with them*, but rather you would like them to explain some exercise techniques to you (whenever suits them).

Working out, from an anecdotal perspective, is good for an inmate's mood and confidence. If you have never really been much of a 'fitness fanatic', consider trying to introduce exercise into your daily routine – it might be one of the best decisions you ever make.

Please note
This section deals with social activities to keep busy, yet you've just been told it's better to work out alone. While, for the most part, those with ASD will find working out alone more rewarding, *some* will prefer a group setting, which is why it has been included in the social activities section.

Jail-based Educational Courses and Group Activities

Another way to pass time, and stimulate your brain, is to get involved in activities and courses offered to inmates. The type and frequency of courses depends on:

- where your prison is (prisons built further from city centres usually have fewer programs on offer)
- funding (right-wing governments tend to place less emphasis on rehabilitation)
- how long you are likely to be in prison
- how the powers-that-be decide to apportion their budget.

Also, the *type* of jail you're in affects the availability, frequency and quality of course/activities offered. Reception jails, for example, rarely offer much in the way of courses or activities. For more information on the differences between facilities, see Chapter 3.

Remand jails
Remand jails often give inmates the chance to demonstrate a willingness to change before being sentenced or being sent to trial, so there may be more course/activities on offer. Usually activities can be split into two types:

1. Courses run by COs.
2. Courses run by outside contractors.

Some examples of CO-run courses:

- anger management
- budgeting
- domestic violence prevention courses
- drug/alcohol intervention programs.

Examples of outside contractor-run courses:

- personal trainers (who teach classes – not just you!)
- first-aid courses
- basic literacy and numeracy
- vocational courses such as:
  - traffic control
  - working safely in the construction industry
  - working in asset maintenance (cleaning operations)
  - working in transport and logistics (warehousing and storage).

Please note
The above courses are examples, based on real experience. Courses will vary from jail to jail.

Reception jails
Reception jails generally offer less in the way of courses and group activities. This is because inmates tend to come and go quickly, so there's less reason to try to engage them with educational

courses. Also, people in reception jails have been sentenced, so the incentive to be the 'model prisoner' is nullified. However, grounds still need to be kept tidy and the prison population fed, so there is work available for inmates. Those who get jobs usually stay in the reception jail longer, so how you feel about reception jails and their 'vibe' should be considered when deciding whether to apply for work. If you do decide to try to get a job, be sure to apply within a week of your arrival at the jail. How you go about applying for these positions is discussed in Chapter 11, Jail Basics.

Placement jails

Placement jails are a conundrum, in terms of activities offered and keeping busy. On the one hand, you are there because you have been sentenced and have a much, much clearer idea of how long you will have to wait until freedom, which for some inmates is years away. On the other hand, *because* you have been sentenced, there are fewer vocational programs on offer. The system's obligation to provide inmates with the ability to demonstrate a desire to change is far less relevant. However, keeping inmates mentally (and physically) stimulated reduces boredom, and that in turn can have a positive 'flow-on' effect to the inmates en masse, such as:

- less drug usage
- less fighting
- enhanced cooperation with the COs
- a more optimistic 'vibe' within the jail.

Senior management are aware of this, and would have all inmates working if they were able to, but they can only do so much with their budget.

KEEPING BUSY – GROUP ACTIVITIES IN PLACEMENT JAIL

As mentioned earlier, courses offered at placement jails are less common. However, there are inmates who *need* to complete certain courses to fulfil requirements set out by the parole board.

Please note

Unless it is a condition of your parole, there are some courses you can't access. There's already a waiting list, so unless you *need* to do the course, don't bother applying. These are courses that focus on issues like domestic violence, the ramifications of recidivist offending, how to get around town when you've lost your licence indefinitely, and so on. Also, don't worry that you may need to do a certain course to be eligible for parole but aren't aware of it – you will be told clearly what is expected of you regarding parole.

Occasionally, placement jails will offer generic courses:

- budgeting
- staying clean from drugs
- fostering healthy relationships.

To make sure you know what's going on, politely ask the COs if anything has come up. Just don't ask them *too* much; about once a month is enough.

WHY BOTHER WITH A COURSE?

If you are not particularly interested in the courses on offer, don't let that deter you. Courses provide a valuable deviation from daily routine. Plus, you will have engaged in some formal socialising in a safe prison environment. Doing courses also helps pass time – the essence of this chapter.

ASD and group-based learning

Group-based activities and ASD don't always go too well together. Fortunately, the educational programs offered are delivered as one would expect them to be – in a classroom setting – complete with chairs, desks, a whiteboard and a teacher, so it won't be an unfamiliar environment. You won't necessarily know many of the other students, and they won't all know each other, because the class consists of inmates from across the jail.

Please note
Inmates from protection will never interact with inmates from mainstream. Both streams have their own class times. Mainstream and protection inmates *never* meet.

Because the class is new to all students, you don't have to find your place in an already established social hierarchy – you're just another inmate. The content of the course won't be difficult. Don't offer help to inmates unless they ask. This could be misconstrued as patronising. If, however, they ask for assistance, help them. It will be genuinely appreciated.

Oval/gym time

Most prisons offer inmates oval and/or gym time about four times a week, but this varies, dependent on whether COs turn up to escort those wanting to go. The unit's COs must stay and watch inmates who don't go the gym/oval. *The gym and oval aren't all they seem*: sometimes more than one unit will attend the oval/gym, so it can become an effective means of exchanging contraband and information. Also, if someone has run afoul of their fellow inmates, it will be down on the oval or in the gym where retribution is carried out. In this regard, it is arguable that the inmate with ASD *shouldn't* make a habit of going to the oval/gym. It's akin to not knowing somebody's PIN – if you don't know, it automatically rules you out if money goes missing. The COs may interview everyone who was down there. If you weren't there, you have no information to give, and can't be accused of divulging any. There are ways to get all the cardio and muscle-building exercise you need right there in the unit's yard.

To summarise

There aren't a lot of prison-organised activities that will keep the inmate with ASD deeply stimulated. However, something is better than nothing, and courses are great for passing the time. The social side isn't difficult. No one really knows who you are – for all they know you could have trained in martial arts. But always remember: while courses or a job can help time go faster, and provide structure, keep in mind your ASD and the propensity for it to cause social disruption – don't let your guard down. And as mentioned before – inmates have long memories. Don't give them anything to remember.

Going Solo

All inmates need time alone, even the ones who get around like they're attached at the hip. Inmates with ASD need alone time more than most, and, fortunately, jail is an environment where alone time can be accessed easily. Many inmates, ASD or not, seek solitude. Socialising in small doses, and small doses only, is not going to make you stand out.

There are ways to keep your mind active, even if you don't have access to your SI(s). Making the time go as fast as possible has its foundation in routine. Even if you don't have a jail job, choose not to work out and avoid courses, routine will still be central to staying as content as possible. Routine helps slow down the racing thoughts and negative ruminations – not completely, but significantly. This portion of the book identifies activities that can form routine for you.

Exercise

For inmates with ASD, working out alone is generally preferable to group workouts. Freedom from social interaction allows maximum focus on the workout, and you won't be the only inmate exercising alone. You will find yourself talking to other inmates about exercise during workouts – swapping advice on technique and so forth. Be sure to engage with other inmates if you exercise regularly – this is how friendships form, over common interests. And we all need friends, regardless of what we might tell ourselves.

Courses

Solo courses are mainly tertiary education or preparation for tertiary education. While behind bars, inmates successfully complete undergraduate degrees, diplomas and, depending on funding, even Master's degrees. Some jails may offer vocational courses, in areas such as metalwork, welding, carpentry, mechanics and so on. Obviously, eligibility is subject to criteria, such as:

- your length of stay
- previous education
- other qualifications you have
- whether you're entitled to funding.

Reading

For some, the word 'reading' is enough to make them feel bored. But the act of reading a book can be surprisingly effective at passing the time, especially if it's an absorbing story. Other benefits from reading are:

- It sends a signal to others that says 'I'm busy and would prefer not to talk'.
- It's a form of both meditation and mindfulness.
- Having a reputation as a quiet inmate who keeps to themselves is beneficial, especially if you show little interest in other inmates' behaviours, like drug-taking, fighting and unit gossip.

There isn't usually a huge range of books to choose from, so you'll have to be flexible. But this can have an upside too. You may find yourself reading something you would have otherwise ignored, diversifying your reading habits and opening the door to new genres and authors. Accessing reading material is discussed in Chapter 11.

Helping people

By definition, helping people is not a solo activity. However, it's included in this section because if you choose to help people with their legal issues, it's mostly either interpreting legal documents or writing legal documents, both of which are, at their core, solo activities. If you are picked out as being intelligent, inmates may ask for your help with:

- understanding legal documents
- interpreting probation and parole correspondence
- writing parole applications
- drafting letters to probation and parole to clarify issues of contention
- writing letters home (some inmates have trouble with all forms of writing and reading)
- corresponding with government departments (such as Social Security)
- any other areas where an inmate is struggling to comprehend what's required of them.

It's not uncommon for inmates have incomplete or inadequate schooling, and they may feel embarrassment about this. Remember never to belittle or express dismay at another person's lack of knowledge – there are plenty of things *you* don't know, too.

The first-timers unit was a hectic cesspit of primarily young men out to prove (to themselves more than anyone else) that they were right at home in jail. Because of this, inmates were reluctant to ask for help, any kind of help, whether it be training tips or help dissecting a complicated legal document. As such, I did very little in the way of helping fellow inmates with the written word. But when I got to the drug rehab unit, where there were only 20 of us, it was a lot easier to suss out who was who and what they were like. My fellow inmates noticed I read a lot, played Scrabble a lot and generally displayed behaviour one could call 'indicative of intelligence'. Naturally, they were curious about how I wound up in maximum security prison, so I told them in two simple but accurate words: drug addiction. This made sense to them because when we were discussing the subculture of the drug world, I was quite obviously not a fraud and had in fact been battling drug dependence since some of my fellow inmates were children.

A few days later, an inmate asked very politely if I could have a look over his parole application, and, if possible, offer him any advice. I looked at what he had and thought, 'I'm definitely going to help this guy – he needs it.' So, we found a quiet corner, I got some paper from my notebook outside my cell, and I asked him some questions about what had happened, why he was here, family background, hardship issues and the like. I had seen on the notice board a piece of paper clearly indicating what the parole board want to know, so following that, we composed his letter. He was grateful, and I turned down his offer to buy me some chocolate on the buy-up. I said, 'Mate, just knowing I helped you is enough for me.' And it was.

I left the unit after I was sentenced, headed to reception jail. But during the four months I was there, I helped about ten people with their parole applications, and they were all very grateful, and, as far as I know, the letters were helpful. I received specific, positive feedback. Inmates respected my willingness to help, but I was never threatened into helping somebody. I guess even the dumbest inmate knows you don't look a gift horse in the mouth.

I continued to help people for the remainder of my sentence, and it always made me feel good. Moreover, it helped pass the time.

Obviously, walking around asking inmates if they need academic help is both strange and patronising. If you are of the intellectual persuasion, it won't take long for it to show. Wait until an inmate asks for help. Until then, just focus on staying busy – watching, listening and learning.

Please note
Having said it's a good idea to help other inmates with legal work, don't do it at the expense of your own legal matters. If you have important matters to attend to, these should always come first.

Walking
Otherwise known as 'cutting laps', this is the process of pacing from one end of the yard to the other. It's healthy, it provides fresh air, and sunlight helps lift your mood. Importantly for the inmate with ASD, the repetitive nature of pacing helps soothe the racing mind and exercise releases feel-good brain chemicals. Lots of inmates pace, alone or in groups. Some spend hours doing it. That alone suggests there's something intrinsically soothing about it.

Writing
Keeping a journal of how you are feeling, or writing short stories or poems is a great creative outlet, and may help identify issues you didn't even consciously know were bothering you. People with ASD can have trouble recognising and articulating how they feel. This can lead to pent-up frustration, and in jail it's imperative this frustration isn't unleashed in a manner that could lead to trouble.

Insulting a tough inmate because they pushed your buttons on a bad day will not end well. Understanding where your negative emotions stem from is very important. Writing can help with this.

Please note
It is important that the only writing done 'in public' (in the yard or unit) is legal or bureaucratic in nature. Save any personal writing for the safety of your cell. If you go around with a notebook, randomly making notes, inmates will suspect you are conducting reconnaissance for the COs.

Drawing

Drawing can help pass the time and, even if you're not a great artist, just the sensation of creating something can be soothing and rewarding. Procuring art materials is not usually difficult and will be explained in Chapter 11. Some inmates are fantastic artists and can be seen working on their creations at their designated table. If you're a gifted artist, inmates won't think you're showing off if you choose to draw outside your cell. Nor will inmates make fun of someone who's just drawing for the sake of it – it's human nature to while away the time making shapes and patterns.

Legal (pre-sentencing)

While on remand, some of your time will be spent on pre-trial or pre-sentencing interaction with your defence team. Regardless of whether you are being privately represented or have a state-funded defence team, you won't see a great deal of them. To them, time is money, and the process of visiting the jail is money wasted.

You may speak on the phone to them more frequently, but for the most part it's just you and your legal documents. However, there are things you can (and should) do prior to your court appearance. For example, if your crime involves a victim (such as the person behind the counter of the store you robbed), consider penning a letter of apology/remorse. This can be given to your legal team, and they can have it passed on to the person. This looks good in the eyes of the judge – they want to see that you *know* what you did was against the law, and you are sorry. If you plan to contest the charge(s), read and reread all the relevant documents. It's better to know something you don't need to, than to need to know something you don't.

After court, you want to be able to look yourself square in the mirror and say, 'I did everything I could to get the best outcome possible.'

Legal (post-sentencing)

Obviously, once you have been sentenced (unless you plan an appeal), the legal side of matters is by and large finished, except for when it comes to the time for parole applications.

Parole applications

If an inmate is sentenced to a term on the low end of the scale (one to three years), dependent upon the jurisdiction, they may be automatically eligible for parole after a percentage of the sentence in served. For everyone else (except those sentenced to life without the possibility of parole), they will begin the process of their parole application at some point. While tedious, it's very necessary. It's like homework – do a bit, then reward yourself with some TV (or whatever relaxes you). Then do a bit more. Trying to tackle it in one go will only frustrate you.

Finally

One of the best ways to help beat boredom while inside is to approach everything you do in a calm, methodical way. Once you have figured out who the more 'seasoned' prisoners are, watch them – you'll see they are never in a hurry, and are meticulous in almost all they do. This is not an accident. The longer you stay inside, the more you realise there *is* no rush, and the *process* of making a cup of tea is as important as the tea itself. Try to slow your mind, so that keeping *busy*, per se, is not high on your agenda.

CHAPTER 11

Jail Basics

Introduction

This chapter examines the pragmatic aspects of jail, such as how to top up your phone account or access the library. This chapter is by no means comprehensive: covering every detail of day-to-day life would be an exhausting and needless process. You will pick things up as you go along. People with ASD usually learn about practical things with relative ease. It's the social angle that can be perplexing and complicated. The *social* basics of jail will be discussed in the next chapter.

Please note
The information here will not be 100 per cent applicable to all jails and/or judicial systems – it's a guide, rather than a manual.

Unit and Cell Allocation

After leaving the watch house, you will go to the remand jail. Here, you will spend a short time (one to three nights) in the *induction unit*, before being sent to the *first-timers unit* (provided, of course, this is your first stint behind bars).

What's a 'unit'? A unit is the building you will live in. It has cells (usually 20–50), a laundry, a kitchen area, phones, the desk where the COs sit, tables and steel chairs welded to the floor for eating, and a communal TV with seating. There will be a communal toilet, and the yard outside will have basic exercise equipment like chin-up bars, dip bars and push-up bars.

When you depart from the reception unit, you will be told very clearly by the COs which unit you have been assigned to. When you arrive at that unit, you will be told which cell is yours.

In-house Induction

Most jails will send you to an induction session not long after your arrival. These sessions are announced over the public address (PA) system, and they will call out your last name (along with others who are new to the unit). These sessions are moderately helpful, albeit brief and delivered with a level of enthusiasm that suggests the CO is doing it for the 10,000th time.

The PA System

The PA system will deliver communal information, such as:

- oval/gym time
- library access
- visits, etc.

The system can be crackly. If you think something might have been mentioned that affects you, ask a CO for clarification. Also, the speaker is quite loud, so if you are startled easily due to ASD, locate the speaker (it will be in a box), and avoid sitting under/near it.

ID Cards

While being processed (see Chapter 6) you will have had your photo taken. This is for your prison identification card. This card will be issued to you when you leave the induction unit, headed to the first-timers unit. You won't be able to hold on to this card; it will be held in your unit, behind the COs' desk. You will need it for security purposes when you move around the jail. When you are due to leave the unit (to go medical/visits, etc.), you will be issued your card. When you get back to your unit, you hand the card back. If you lose or mess up your ID card, a small amount of money will be taken from your prison account to replace it.

The Library

Often, books arrive on a small cart pushed from unit to unit by an inmate who works in the library. Because only so many books can fit on said cart, there is a limit to how many books are on offer at any given time. This may initially frustrate the inmate with ASD. However, you can ask the inmate pushing the cart to look for specific books for you from the main library. They will be happy to do this; just remember to always use your manners.

Phone Accounts

Once you get to a unit, watch your fellow inmates. The seasoned ones will be quick to grab specific forms from the communal form rack, located near the desk where the COs sit. One of these forms allows you to write down a list of people who you want on your phone account. The number of contacts is generally limited to ten, but that's usually enough to allow you contact with family, friends and your legal team. Numbers can also be removed if they become obsolete. To fill in this form, use the pen you got in your bed pack (see Chapter 6). The people you listed will be contacted by the prison and their consent is needed for their number to go onto your phone account.

Jail bureaucracy is slow. It's important the inmate with ASD remembers this. Those numbers *will* go onto your phone account, or you will be offered an explanation as to why they didn't. The only time phone numbers *don't* go onto your account is when the number isn't answered after multiple attempts, or the person says 'no' to being contacted. If this is the case, you will be notified – usually the form will be sent back to you via the mail (mail will be explained later in this chapter).

To fill in the form adequately, you will need to remember the following about the person(s) you want to have on your phone account:

- full name
- phone number (obviously)
- address.

They will also ask for a description of 'your relationship to the person' (friend, brother, lawyer, etc).

To access your phone account, enter your prison number (which will have been allocated to you from day dot and won't change – you will learn it quickly). Once you have entered your prison number, you will be asked to enter a PIN. You will have selected this PIN during processing (see Chapter 6).

Once into your account, select a person to call from your list of numbers and that's it. You'll be able to hear the voices of those you miss most.

Phone calls will almost always be timed, and when that time is up (usually 10–15 minutes), you can't call again from that particular phone for a certain amount of time.

Some units have more than one phone, so you can 'bounce' between phones. However, this is not necessarily a good *social* practice. Only do this when things are slow, like mid-afternoon when people have retreated to their cells for a nap.

Please note

All calls (except for calls to your legal team) are monitored and recorded, so watch what you say if you plan to contest the charges against you. Also, be very careful what you say regarding activity in the unit; that is, *never* mention anything about drug activity or anything to do with any clandestine behaviour, regardless of how trivial it may seem. Remember – loose lips sink ships.

Phone Money

You will need money in your phone account to make calls. Except for your 'reception call' (see Chapter 6), jails don't give you free calls to friends and loved ones. To put money onto your phone account you submit a form, one giving permission for the jail to take $X from your *prison account* (see below) and transfer it onto your phone account. This is something you would generally do weekly.

Prison Account

Your prison account is as it sounds – your own 'bank account' for use exclusively within the confines of the jail system. It works like this: the government will send you a small 'hygiene allowance' every week, so *everyone* can shave, wash their hair, clean their teeth and soap their bodies. This is not a large allowance. If you have a prison job, you will be paid (very little compared with the outside world – but it *is* jail, what do you expect?). This money will also go into your account. Then there's the option of a friend or loved one sending you money. This is how most inmates get the bulk of their funds.

Money can be put into your prison account in the following ways:

- Sending in a money order.
- Sending in a cheque (this can take longer to process).
- Sending in cash (not recommended but usually works).
- Somebody physically visits the jail and hands a money order, cheque or cash to the front desk.

When money has entered your account, you will be notified via a numbered receipt, given to you during mail distribution in the afternoon.

Please note
Prison accounts are taken seriously by the COs. They appreciate the value of money too, so will make a genuine effort to rectify any problems. Just be patient. It can be frustrating dealing with money issues, but you'll get a lot further if you keep your cool.

Sending Mail

You will have been issued with a couple of pre-paid envelopes, some writing paper and a pen in your bed pack, so you can start sending mail straight away.

Please note
Except for legal mail, all mail (both outgoing and incoming) will be read (or at least skimmed) by the COs. So, although theoretically free to write what you want, it's probably best you *don't* write to your mate, telling them how much you want to beat up a particular CO or your intricate escape plans.

There will be a clearly marked tray into which you put mail you want sent out (don't seal the envelope – they read it, remember).

Receiving Mail

In the afternoon, the COs will call out 'mail' and inmates will congregate around the COs' desk. COs call out last names, but don't stress if you miss the mail call – they are obliged by law to ensure inmates receive their mail, so they will hold it for you. Legal mail must be signed for, and you must open the envelope in front of the COs and shake it (to show it doesn't contain contraband).

Buy-ups (or 'Canteen')

Jails allow inmates access to a limited (but adequate) list of items one could find in a supermarket. This includes things like:

- food staples (cereal, noodles, tuna, cheese, etc.)
- cooking aids (chicken stock cubes, soy sauce, garlic granules, etc.)
- sweet food (chocolate, lollies, biscuits, etc.)
- toiletries (toothpaste, shampoo, mouthwash, nail clippers, etc.)
- stationery (pre-paid envelopes, notebooks, pens, etc.)
- clothes (underwear, socks and singlets/vests)
- tokens (these are sold to inmates for cold cans of soft drink/soda from the communal vending machine).

There's a designated day when people fill in and submit their buy-up forms. You will learn quickly what day buy-ups are due, as you will see other inmates filling in their forms and the COs will remind inmates during headcount to have their form handed in to the COs' desk by day's end. There will be a limit to how much you can spend each week, but the amount will be more than enough to provide you with an adequate amount of goods. Remember to get that form in by the end of the day, because you won't be able to submit it late.

You can ask the COs for an account balance any time during the week, and they will usually be compliant. Remember your manners, don't pester the COs and don't ask for a balance when they are obviously busy.

Buy-up arrives about five days after the forms are submitted, and if for some reason you are not there (you may have court or a medical appointment or class), the COs will keep it locked away for you.

'Sales to Prisoner' (STP) Purchases

There are items that a jail may allow inmates to purchase, but that don't appear on the regular 'buy-up' forms. These are known as STP purchases. These include items such as:

- hair clippers
- watches
- crucifixes
- portable CD players (batteries are on the normal buy-up)
- CDs
- radios
- alarm clocks
- kettles
- shoes (trainers)
- sporting goods (boxing gloves and pads)
- more pharmacy items (dental floss, multi-vitamins)
- more stationery items (coloured pencils, sketch pads, magazines, etc.).

Obviously, this list is not exhaustive, and some jails won't have as many items to choose from. This is a guide only. A list of magazines, CDs and other STP items should be available in or near the communal form rack. If there appears to be no such list, explain to a CO what you are looking for and they will be able to either locate the list or print out a new one. Expect to wait up to four weeks for the items, though some items arrive quicker.

Visits

With visits, the onus is on the people wanting to visit you – they must either download (or collect from the jail itself) the requisite forms needed so they can be vetted and approved. They are also responsible for *booking* the visit. This is done via phone – tell them to obtain contact details from the internet. The jail usually needs about a week's notice for visits. Jails appreciate that, for inmates, visits can be very important. Therefore, they are usually helpful and accommodating to your people when they ring to book a visit.

Different jails have different visiting times, and the duration of visits can vary. If you're anxious about a visit and would like confirmation in the morning that your visitors are booked in, ask a CO to check the visit list for that day. Once you've got confirmation, you just wait until you hear 'Afternoon visits! Repeat, afternoon visits are up!' (or 'Morning visits', as the case may be.) That's your cue to ask for your ID card (never leave home without it!) and make your way to visits.

Different types of visits

There are two types of visits. The first is a 'contact' visit, where hugging and touching is permitted. This is only to an extent – COs wander among the tables where inmates sit with their people, and cameras are filming everything. The primary reason for the heavy presence of COs is to watch for the passing of contraband to the inmate (drugs) or from the inmate to a visitor (sensitive written information.)

The secondary reason is to stop inmates getting too physically engaged with the visitor if they happen to be a partner or lover. Sexually deprived inmates can get frisky. This type of visit can be good for many inmates with ASD, because the tactile sensation(s) of being able to hug, touch and smell your loved ones can do wonders for your feelings of happiness and hope.

Provided you have no history of violence with your family, and you haven't come to the attention of the prison authorities over drugs, you should be able to get approval to see your family on a contact visit relatively quickly (expect it to take about a month).

The second type of visit
If you can't have a contact visit, you may have to settle for a non-contact visit. Sometimes, non-contact visits are offered to people who have missed the cut-off date for a particular visiting day, but the jail offers them a non-contact visit to try to be accommodating. This is an example of the jail helping facilitate things that are important to inmates.

Non-contact visits work as you would expect them to: a small booth, semi-private, with either a mesh hole to speak/listen through or a telephone on both sides of the perspex separating you. You have probably seen this type of set-up in a film or on TV. They are a lot less intimate, but you can see your visitor, and look into their eyes, and you get to speak much longer than the timed phone calls.

> **Please note**
> Even though there is a zero per cent chance of contraband
> being passed from visitor to inmate during non-contact visits,
> that doesn't mean you can request a non-contact visit in the
> hope your people will be processed and approved faster. It
> doesn't work like that. Everyone is processed the same way.

The Unexpected Visit

You may one day be told you have a visit when you are not expecting one. If this happens, nine times out of ten it's the police. You
will have to go to the visiting area, but my advice is simply to
refuse to comment and walk out. *You do not want to be seen
talking to the police for more than a couple of minutes. This cannot
be stressed hard enough.*

Usually, the police are there to talk to more than one inmate,
so there are others waiting to go in. They know how long each
person stays in there. Inmates will not trust you if you spend time
chatting amicably with the COs. Imagine how they will respond
if word gets out you were having a nice long chat with the police.
Go in, declare your intention to remain silent, and walk out.

Work

Many inmates seek to pass the time and earn a bit of snack money
by working while incarcerated. Applying for a job is simple. The
first step is getting the correct form from the form rack. There
isn't a long list of jobs to choose from, and most of them are in:

- gardening
- the laundry (industrial size)

- the kitchen
- industries.

Industries refers to basic metal (or 'shop') work. Getting a job isn't difficult, and activities that help pass the time while inside are priceless. There are a few 'specialised' positions, usually reserved for inmates who have been in the jail a long time. These are jobs like working in the library, officially helping other inmates with parole, working in the DU, sorting clothes and so on. There is also the option of working *within* your unit:

- laundry worker (washing inmates' clothes)
- kitchen worker (handing out meals, distributing fruit, cereal, condiments, etc.)
- cleaner (either inside sweeping/mopping or responsible for keeping the yard tidy).

To apply for these internal, unit-based positions, get the requisite form. It will most likely be a separate form from the one asking for work outside the unit. If you are successful in getting a job in the industrial laundry, kitchen, industries or gardening crew, you *may* have to move units. Jails often keep workers housed together. If you have established a group of friends, and you are comfortable in your current unit, you should probably apply for in-unit work, rather than risk moving units and having to go through the process of getting to know people again.

Access to Education

Educational programs on offer will depend significantly on the *type* of jail you are in. However, finding out about courses and the application process is the same in each jail. Go (again!) to the form rack and look for one that directly allows you to apply for classes, or, failing that, use the 'general request' form. This is a covers-all-bases form – you'll be surprised how many times an unexpected question pops up.

On the general request form, state your interest in what programs they have on offer. You should be called to the education block, and a CO will explain what's available and when.

Please note
Taking a class is fine if you don't have any 'enemies' around the jail. However, if you have stepped on someone's toes, and had to move units, don't risk bumping into them down at the education block. *Safety must always come first.*

Breaches

A 'breach' is like getting a citation from a police officer. COs give them to inmates when they break prison rules. If a serious incident occurs (like a murder, or a CO is assaulted), there will be a police investigation. For other incidents, they're dealt with 'in-house' through breaches.

If breached, you will be given the opportunity to give your side of events. The CO in charge of that sector of the prison (a more senior CO) will make a judgement call (which can be appealed) and then issue a punishment. This may be minor, like a warning or losing your television for a few days/nights; for more serious indiscretions, inmates will be 'sentenced' to time in the DU.

The DU/Solitary Confinement

This is where people go to be punished. These units are smaller (often 30 cells or fewer for a 1000-bed jail), and the cells are very sparse. It's just a bed, toilet and sink. No radio, no TV, and whether they have books depends on the jail. Some jails offer only religious texts.

The most common reasons for DU time are: fighting with other inmates (most common), being caught with drugs/drug paraphernalia (next most common) or assaulting or threatening a CO (infrequent).

If you are caught fighting, you get hauled to medical for a check-up, then to the DU.

There is strict protocol in the DU about where/how you stand when they open the door, and any deviation will result in COs swiftly enforcing compliance. People with ASD can respond intensely when backed into a corner, and you may feel this way in the DU. However, *you must keep it together.* Fighting will make it significantly worse.

I thought quite a bit about what I should say regarding the DU, wondering about the most effective way to communicate not what it is (that's very straightforward), but rather how to cope if you're sent there.

I decided the best way would be to explain how I coped, because I can't give concrete advice for Aspies on this one – we're too idiosyncratic, and the way people handle the DU varies wildly.

I was 'sentenced' to six nights for getting caught holding a small amount of tobacco, which, like everyone else, I had saved when smoking was officially outlawed.

The breach involved me and me only, so there was no external social factor to assimilate, which meant I was able to focus on getting through the DU time, instead of worrying about whether I had inadvertently pissed someone off. That was important to me.

The first night they forgot to switch out the lights (unlike normal cells, the light switch is on the outside of the door – inmates have no control over the light). I tied my t-shirt around my head to create the illusion of darkness.

There's often a lot of noise, which is frustrating because the best way to pass the time is by sleeping. But other inmates talk to each other, and it echoes. And you can't tell them to shut up, because if you do, they'll ask your name and unit number; failing to tell them makes you look scared, and then they'll hound you deliberately. Telling them means there's a real chance details of the altercation will make it back to your unit, and one of the inmates in the DU with you might have a brother or cousin in your unit, and before you know it there's trouble. So just put up and shut up.

This applies to the COs too. The unlocking of my tiny (but sunlit) yard was a tedious process, but compliance is by far the best option. I heard a guy argue with a screw in the DU and, to put it simply, I doubt he'll do it again anytime soon.

By the fifth day I was well and truly over it – tired but unable to sleep, deeply bored and hungry because although they bring you three meals a day, I was used to eating surplus food from my buy-up. I kept up my muscle training at least, and that seemed to help. I got a song stuck in my head, but instead of irritating me, it gave me strength. I thought: one day I'll be out of here. Not just the DU, but jail altogether. I would 'play' the song in my head, and it helped me focus on getting through the long hours. And I would spare a thought for some of the boys who had been there two, sometimes three weeks. My *brain was hurting after six nights – I can only speculate as to how 20 nights must feel. Truly horrible, I imagine.*

Play by the rules, and all being well, you won't even go to the DU, but if you do, hopefully this first-person account helps somewhat.

Tips for coping in the DU:

- Cooperate fully with COs.
- Keep the cell clean – it can get surprisingly dirty.
- Shower regularly.
- If you work out, do so in the DU (even if it's a shorter version of your usual routine).
- *Don't* get into verbal spats with the other inmates, even though you can't see them (and vice versa).
- If you are familiar with mindfulness, meditation or any self-administered relaxation techniques, use these.
- If you have access to reading material, take advantage.
- Remember – everyone is doing it hard in the DU, so try to be tolerant.

Urine Tests

As part of the zero-tolerance approach, random drug-testing is used in jails. They give you about 45 minutes to produce a sample. If it comes up positive in the cup, the sample is tagged, bagged and sent for analysis. Punishment is usually time in the DU.

Often, they target inmates who *don't* do drugs. This is quite deliberate. Most units have a set of COs who 'rotate' through on a weekly basis, so they start to get to know the prisoners. When a senior CO asks for the unit to be targeted, the regular COs want to look like they're running a tight ship, so they choose someone they believe is unlikely to test positive.

Failure to produce urine in the allotted time is considered a 'dirty' (or positive) reading. Obnoxiously, this can have a negative effect on being granted parole, so, if you suffer from anxiety when urinating near others, try to address this *prior* to your incarceration. To learn more about how to handle this situation, see the urine tests (UTs) section in Chapter 15.

Preparing for the Day (What to Bring Out of Your Cell)

As mentioned in Chapter 8, prepare what you are going to bring out for the day *before* unlock, not during it. An example of what you may want to bring out:

- a pen
- some paper
- noodles/tuna or any other 'snack' food (especially if you are working out)
- tokens
- any workout 'equipment' (towel, bottle of water)
- any cooking things you might use (like soy sauce or salad dressing)
- any documents you might need – for example, if you are doing an education course and you have a folder for it.

Your property will sit either on the floor near your door, in the 'pigeon hole' (a small box-like space for ventilation that is in the wall next to your cell), or under your communal table (the same table you sit and eat at).

Don't worry – it's very unlikely anyone will steal from it.

It's because of the golden rule (do unto others as you would have them do unto you), and no inmate wants to be known as a petty thief. Make sure all your things come back in with you at night.

Laundry

Laundry usually works like this: in a two-storey unit, Monday, Wednesday and Friday will be upstairs wash day. Tuesday, Thursday and Saturday is downstairs. Sunday is generally reserved for inmates to do their own washing.

There will be a laundry worker responsible for making sure the washing gets done. Trust this person – they will know what they are doing. Just make sure you only wash what you need to (there can be quite a lot of obsessive–compulsive behaviour in jail), and don't bug the laundry worker about whether your laundry's done yet. Also, *don't try to sneak your bag into the pile when it isn't your floor's wash day.* People can be assaulted for this.

Make sure your laundry bag (which will have been given to you in your bed pack upon arrival) is clearly marked with your initials or cell number.

Once washed, your clothes are tumble-dried before being sealed back up in your bag and placed somewhere obvious, like on the seats where the communal television is. Your bedding (including your duvet) is your responsibility to wash. Once a week is considered normal. Any more frequent than that, and you might antagonise the laundry worker.

Extra Clothes

Sometimes the clothes you were issued upon arrival don't fit too well, or are damaged, or get damaged, or somebody accidently picks up your jumper, thinking it belongs to them, and off it goes – there are multiple reasons why you may need to get some replacement clothing.

The first thing to do is politely ask the laundry workers if they have any spares of what you need. If they don't have what you need, there is a form that you can use to request garments (except for underwear and socks – you purchase them on buy-up). Clothes will usually arrive on the same day as buy-up.

Showering

Depending on the age, design and protocol of a jail, there may be a communal showering block, or you may have a shower in your cell. For inmates with ASD, the concept of group showers will be daunting. Remember this – it's daunting for *everyone* who is in jail for the first time. You will cope with communal showers. They are almost always 'partitioned', at least to an extent, so it isn't necessarily 20 naked men (or women) in one big shower block, with no privacy at all. If the showers are communal, and it bothers you, try to get in and out of there as quickly as possible, but not at the expense of hygiene – no one likes an unwashed inmate who you can *smell* is unwashed. Hopefully you will land in a jail that has a shower in each cell. Showers may also be timed, so if you enjoy long showers, accept you may lose this luxury.

Tattoos

In jail lots of inmates have tattoos. Most of these will have been created either in a professional studio or by a 'backyard' tattooist.

Some of them will have been created while behind bars – inmates are ingenious at improvising what they can't get legitimately. There's no need to explain how tattoo-guns are made – just know they're out there. Tattoos can also be used to signify membership or affiliation to a certain group. There are health hazards associated with jailhouse tattooing. Because inmates lack access to clean tattoo needles, alcoholic swabs and proper tattooing ink, getting a tattoo while inside could lead to:

- Hepatitis C
- HIV
- Infection (from ink that isn't compatible with human skin).

Aside from these potential threats, you could also be breached if caught. Also, while some jail tattooists are pretty good, there are others who, well, aren't. It's a gamble you probably shouldn't take.

Risk Assessment Score

The COs are there to keep order and provide a level of security for all inmates. One of the tools they use is a 'score' (or rating) that indicates how dangerous an inmate is perceived to be. This is based on the nature of the crime for which they are doing time, their criminal history and notes on their behaviour since they have been incarcerated. Sometimes you can ask to see your 'score'; other times it's off limits. It depends on why you want to see it and whether the COs deem the request to be reasonable. Your 'score' can affect things like eligibility for transferring to the residential part of the jail, where/if you can work and parole applications. An inmate's risk assessment score can change with time and good behaviour.

Residential Accommodation

In Chapter 3, residential accommodation, or 'res', was briefly mentioned. Akin to a small village *within* the confines of the perimeter walls, res generally houses 300–500 inmates in accommodation that, while like everyday units, is more flexible and allows the inmate more freedom and responsibility. Res can offer:

- The privilege to come and go from your cell as you please, because you have your own key.
- Inmates share a 'house' with four or five others.
- They have a communal kitchen.
- Inmates can stroll around the facility, which is much bigger than the yard of a standard unit.
- Res often has a library and its own education block, along with more frequent access to the gym and oval.

However, for the inmate with ASD, res is almost certainly a bad idea. For more information on *why* this is the case, see the section on res in Chapter 3. However, if you *still* think res is for you, getting there is simply a matter of filling in the requisite form and waiting. Spots come up often, as inmates are regularly kicked out of res for failing urine tests, engaging in other drug-related behaviour or fighting.

Weekly Inspections

Once a week (on the same day), the COs will do an inspection of the unit, including your cell. This is different to 'ramping', or 'tossing' a cell, which refers to the procedure of COs conducting random searches to keep inmates in line. In a weekly inspection, the whole unit is assessed by senior COs for cleanliness and compliance with jail policy. As for your cell, you need to take the sheets and duvet and fold them neatly on your bed. Also, tidy up any general clutter and sweep and mop your floor. Equipment for sweeping and mopping will be made available to you on the morning of the inspection, and cell doors are left open longer to allow everyone time to get their cells clean.

'Failing' an inspection is not a big deal – a CO will simply ask you to 'take down this or that' or 'give that sink a better scrub', etc. They have hundreds of cells to look at; they don't waste much time in each one.

Random Searches

As mentioned above, COs can and do search cells thoroughly. It varies: it can be a targeted search of one or more cells, a random search of one or more cells or the searching of the whole unit, including every cell. It happens more in remand jails than placement jails because there are more drugs and contraband in remand jails (see Chapters 3 and 9 for more detail on this).

In some jurisdictions, policy dictates the inmate be present for the search, as a witness. This is done in more progressive jails to help keep things on an even keel and avoid corruption, like 'planting' contraband in an inmate's cell. If it is done this way, wait to be called in from the yard (where you will have been instructed to go en masse) and stand by quietly as they conduct their search.

If it's done the other way, and you're stuck out in the yard, you can assume all is good if they *don't* call out your name and ask you to go inside with them to your cell.

> **Please note**
> The COs *may* ask that you undergo a strip search. *Don't worry – it will be the same sort of non-invasive search you will have been through when you came into jail* (see Chapter 2). Ramping is not a stressful event – unless you have something to hide. So, if you do, always keep in the back of your mind the possibility that the authorities could catch you unawares.

Legal Documents

Inmates accumulate a good deal of legal paperwork during their stay behind bars. This is especially applicable for people on remand (those awaiting sentencing or trial). Try to keep all your documents together. Purchase an A4-sized envelope (available on buy-up) and keep all your pertinent legal papers together. This is especially applicable to the inmate with ASD, as it will help you feel in control and lower anxiety levels. If you take any legal documents outside your cell, *make sure you bring them back in with you!* Losing valuable legal documents is not conducive to relaxation.

Most jails will have a legal section in their libraries, so you can work on your defence, seek confirmation of legal facts and so on. How to access the legal library varies from jail to jail, so if it isn't clear, ask an inmate first, and if they don't know, ask a CO.

The Riot Squad

The riot squad is just what it sounds like – a team of COs who have had extra training in the field of crowd control/rioting. These guys are not called if a regular fight breaks out (those are dealt with by standard COs), but rather when the COs lose control of a unit (rare), are *worried* about losing control of a unit (more likely) or they must deal with a prisoner with a history of violence against COs (most likely).

If you find yourself in a situation where the riot squad enters, and they appear intent on subduing every inmate (as opposed to just the non-compliant inmate), the best thing you can do is lie on the floor and put your hands over your head, with your fingers interlaced. By voluntarily putting yourself in this submissive position, you minimise the risk of being manhandled in a painful/ and or demeaning manner.

Please note
The riot squad is rarely deployed, but when they are, they mean business. So, unless you *want* to get hurt, cooperate.

Canines

Some people with ASD can have a fear of dogs, or a strong aversion to the sound of a dog barking. The sound is like the cliché 'nails down the chalkboard', only much more intense. This is mentioned because while in jail you will more than likely see (and hear) dogs after a fight has broken out and the COs need to restore order.

There are COs who have been assigned to work with a trained canine, usually a German Shepherd or Rottweiler. These dogs are never set upon inmates, at least not deliberately. If someone is dumb enough to try to attack a CO while the dog is present, and somehow they make it past all the other COs, then maybe a dog will be used to subdue an inmate. They do bark and carry on, however, and sometimes you may wonder why they can't train them to shut up.

Fortunately, you will never have to be around dogs for long. Once the melee has calmed down, the dogs are taken away quickly. There isn't much you can do if you have a strong dislike of dogs or their barking, but at the risk of being repetitive – forewarned is forearmed.

Staff Training

It's routine for jails to have a half-day lockdown once a week, almost always on the same day at the same time. What may vary, however, is when you are let out again. Generally, staff training is in the morning, so you will be let out as usual to have breakfast, then about an hour after unlock, you will go back into your cells. Ensure that if you have taken anything out with you, it comes back in. It can be very frustrating to be able to see your book sitting on your table, only metres away, with no way in the world to get it. These lockdowns last no less than two hours and no longer than five, so it's a good opportunity for some quiet time or extra sleep.

Smoking

It's becoming less common for smoking to be permitted in correctional facilities. Of course, there are exceptions for every rule. If the jail you are housed in *is* a smoking facility, here is a basic rundown about tobacco in jail. You will be able to buy your smoking products on the buy-up form, but what you *won't* be able to get is a lighter or matches. You light your cigarettes in the yard, using a device like a car's cigarette lighter – a coil that burns red hot. It's triggered by a button and set in a small hole, a centimetre or so deep, so people can't burn themselves. You are not allowed to smoke in the unit or in your cell, although this rule gets broken. Inmates have a lot of time to think things through, and they have devised ways to light their cigarettes without matches or a lighter.

If you are a non-smoker, and you wind up in a jail that allows smoking, don't start the habit. It's expensive and pointless.

Cameras

One of the most effective ways in which COs can maintain law and order, considering they are vastly outnumbered, is via cameras. Cameras are manned during the day. You can see them move. They aren't like cameras in a department store, which act as deterrents – these cameras are actively looking for inmates breaking rules. There are cameras on the walkways, cameras at all the gates, cameras in the yard of the unit and cameras *inside* the unit: a lot of cameras, and not just for show.

Cameras are not allowed in individual cells, although there's a bit more to it than that. Cameras can be placed in designated double-up cells. These are cells with bunkbeds, and two sets of shelving space. The size of the cell is bigger too. They put cameras in these cells so they have a much better chance of knowing what really happened if an inmate winds up getting seriously hurt. They are also used in cells in the medical wing, so staff can monitor inmates for physical and mental health reasons.

If you are in a cell with a camera, *don't* put wet toilet paper or anything over the lens to obstruct the view. The COs will notice quickly, and they won't be amused.

Intercoms

Each cell will come equipped with a 'medical emergency intercom'. This is a red button that should be pushed only for legitimate reasons. Bothering COs with trivial complaints isn't looked upon favourably.

In the Bronx units, it's best to avoid using the intercom, unless you really are having a medical emergency, or if you're doubled-up and your cellmate is having a medical emergency. The reason you should exercise restraint regarding the emergency intercom is because other inmates can hear the button being pushed, and some of the less sensible/paranoid inmates may misconstrue the communication as you 'dobbing' in someone for something. Of course, this is ludicrous. If one really *were* a jailhouse snitch, this would be a stupid and ineffective means of communication with the authorities. But inmates don't always follow logic – so try to avoid using the emergency intercom unless you absolutely must.

Lockdowns

Lockdowns were mentioned earlier in the chapter, in the section titled 'Staff Training'. But lockdowns can occur for other reasons. These include (but are not limited) to:

- After a more serious fight in the unit.
- If the jail is having construction work done (this may not affect the whole jail).
- If there has been serious trouble in another unit, such as a riot. All other inmates jail-wide are locked down to prevent the uprising from spreading.
- If a CO is seriously assaulted.

- If a high-profile inmate is coming in/leaving and there's media attention.
- If an ambulance must be called into the centre.
- If the weather poses risk for inmates. For example, if a storm is directly above the jail.
- Disease control – if an infection (like measles) is detected. A confined, highly populated area like a prison is at risk of mass infection, so all inmate movement is restricted/ monitored. If this happens, and you are locked down for days, meals are brought to you along with mail and medication.
- Strike action – this is more common in privately run jails, and when it does happen a skeleton crew of staff run the jail. Strike action is rare and doesn't last long if it occurs at all.
- If a prisoner is missing.
- If a prisoner or prisoners have gotten onto the roof of one of the buildings, or another restricted area.

Most of the time the COs will let inmates know what's going on, but they are under no obligation to do so, so be polite and don't pester them. They will come and check on inmates periodically, as per night-time protocol.

Sometimes food may be late, but you will be fed. If you are due in court, they will know about it and take the appropriate measures. No one will be penalised in court because a lockdown prevented them from appearing in person.

For inmates with ASD, lockdowns can provide extended downtime. If you have a close relationship with a loved one or friend, and you know they might be worried because they haven't heard from you, don't stress too much – your people can check the internet or ring the facility, and once they've established that the person is a legitimate contact of yours, the operator can explain exactly what's happening.

Homemade Weapons

Although jail isn't exactly like it's portrayed in popular culture, there is one area where Hollywood has got it right, and that's the depiction of 'homemade' weapons. Because inmates will always need a basic level of healthcare, toothbrushes are less a privilege and more a right. So is plastic cutlery. And these two items (along with others) can be fashioned into potentially deadly weapons with relative ease. There is very little authorities can do about this, as these weapons can be made fast, passed from inmate to inmate and hidden quickly and efficiently.

Obviously, there are penalties if you are caught with homemade weapons. They can range from a warning, or minor breach, right up to an 'outside charge', which could add time to your sentence.

If you are allocated a cell and find a homemade weapon hidden in there (presumably from the last inmate), quietly dispose of it. Don't tell other inmates, and obviously don't tell the COs. Just throw it in a communal bin when you get a chance.

Navigating the Jail

Jails are essentially small villages and, like a small village, you will learn the layout quickly. Finding different buildings is straightforward. There is (usually) clear signage, but ask another inmate if you find yourself confused. You *can* ask a CO for directions but if there are a few other inmates around, *don't ask the CO.* Remember, you are being watched by cameras, so try not to linger, or stand there for five minutes yelling out to a friend in a different part of the jail.

When it comes to movement, you can take your time, just don't go somewhere you shouldn't, or spend too much time conversing with other inmates. Try to keep a balance between toeing the line and appearing not to care.

A Final Note

The list of aspects of jail life given in this chapter is by no means definitive – to cover *every* aspect of prison life would take a long time. The issues mentioned are ones that it is helpful to know about prior to incarceration. There will inevitably be issues to face in your daily jail travels that *weren't* addressed. For these, the best advice is this:

- Watch and wait (don't dive right in).
- Try not to do anything that draws attention to yourself.
- Don't make assumptions.
- Respect those around you.
- Remember the difference between a right and a privilege.
- Don't let your ASD be your defining characteristic – you are much more than a walking diagnosis.

Remember, you are strong. You are unique. You will adapt and learn. You have as much right to dignity and quality of life as anybody else. You will leave jail behind, literally, or in the case of life sentences, you will learn to live with your mind free.

Part 3
Social Navigation

The preceding chapters looked at the pragmatic side of jail, but it's the *social* dynamic which poses the greatest challenge to inmates with ASD. ASD will affect both how you approach jail life and how you cope with it. Obviously, jail won't be the first time you have experienced negative thoughts, emotions or feelings triggered by interaction with other people. What will be new, however, is the experience of being in an environment which you cannot simply leave if things get a bit too much.

The following chapters focus specifically on what constitutes positive inmate behaviour, how best to interact with fellow inmates and jail staff, ways to avoid confrontation, how to handle it if it does arise, and coping mechanisms to ease stress. Jail is something *everybody* can learn to live with. There are times when it will feel like your sentence stretches out before you like a never-ending highway. There are also times when you will feel contentment, excitement and levity. Many people come out of jail as more rounded, worldly individuals with a new-found appreciation of freedom and what that really means. Before that time comes, you will be dealing with an intense and often confusing environment. This portion of the text is written to help you feel safe and 'naturalised' inside jail – free from intimidation and bullying, and capable of rising above daily frustrations so they don't come to define the time you spent inside.

CHAPTER 12

General Social Advice

Introduction

For many neurotypical inmates, the social side of jail poses few challenges, especially if they have, like most of the prison population, come to be inside because of addiction. Some subcultures even see jail as a 'rite of passage'. However, if you have ASD, and have encountered social problems related to it, such as bullying, teasing, exclusion and saying 'the wrong thing at the wrong time', jail is likely to be challenging. This doesn't mean you won't be able to adapt and find your place in the social hierarchy behind bars, even if this place is at the lower end of the 'popularity' spectrum. Ask yourself: do you really care? This book is about *minimising* negative experiences, not *maximising* your social standing in an environment that, for most people, comprises a small percentage of their lifetime.

Once you're back in the free world, all the nonsense of jail is irrelevant. You may change temporarily while inside in order to cope, but once you are out of jail, you can relax and feel free to be who you really are. Traits you do bring out with you could be good ones: patience, strength and a new-found respect for freedom.

Please note
This chapter cannot possibly address all the issues you could face during your time behind bars. Instead, key issues are raised, ones that, from an anecdotal perspective, are more likely to present than others. But the general principles of personal conduct remain the same across the board and are applicable to a multitude of situations.

Enforced Socialising

Frustratingly, the inmate with ASD doesn't have much choice but to socialise because of the confined nature of jails. There are some inmates (not necessarily diagnosed with ASD) who play up to the point they are permanently segregated from the entire prison population. This is an extreme measure to take, and would be significantly more difficult to endure compared with engaging in minimal, but necessary, socialising. Here, we look at socialising while in jail from a practical standpoint, so that you can enter the prison environment with a degree of confidence.

While in placement jail, in a Bronx unit, one of the things I noticed, one of the things that really stood out to me, was the behaviour of another inmate who sat at the table I was allocated to. This guy would be loud, brash and even jokingly insult some of the tougher men in the unit. It was bewildering. He would say something offensive, and I'd be thinking, 'Okay, he's pushed it too far, surely the guy he's speaking to isn't gonna like this. I think this is going to end badly.' Then – nothing. Nothing would happen. The other inmate would laugh, ignore him or insult him back. Meanwhile I'm sitting there, bewildered, thinking, 'If that was me who had said that, I would expect to be punched.' And it's not like this inmate was particularly tough, or hardened. He was overweight, about 22 or 23 and not particularly bright. But somehow it was like he could see social barriers, as one can see road markings. He would get close to the line, but not cross it. Or like there was a little voice inside him telling him when to back down and when he could push it.

It was fascinating to watch. And it was the antithesis of my own social radar, which seemed to malfunction regularly. That was one of the first times I saw just how much my Asperger's could separate me from other inmates. I also knew I needed to learn quickly and, when in doubt, keep my mouth shut.

The Opinionated Inmate

Unlike the individual described in the anecdote above, it's very important the inmate with ASD *isn't* loud, brash and confrontational. Having said that, anyone, not just those with ASD, has a propensity to become confrontational if their 'hot button' is pushed. We all have topics we feel strongly about. In jail, it's best to avoid talking about these. If an inmate says something stupid, and you know for sure they're wrong, just let it go. If they are a friend and you are having an amicable discussion, you can challenge them. Otherwise, it really isn't worth it. Do you want to create tension just to prove a point to someone you barely know? This also includes having strong or overt opinions about any topic. Espousing your feelings about this, that or the next is bad form. Remember:

- You don't know how others may feel about the topic.
- Jail is not the place to try to 'educate' people.
- Carrying on and on about something may result in physical confrontation.

The Brainy Inmate

Inmates with ASD may find themselves at a loose end intellectually. As mentioned in Chapter 10, one of the ways to keep your brain active is to participate in classes. If you do, don't be a 'know-it-all', or belittle another inmate whose intelligence isn't akin to yours. It would also be a mistake to say something insulting using big words and assume the inmate doesn't understand what you said. Never underestimate a person's intelligence. Inmates quickly identify those who are more intellectually inclined and, though they may respect this, it won't intimidate them. Reserve your smarts for helping people with parole applications and other legal documents. This will help you gain friends. Being intellectually arrogant, and overtly so, will help you gain a black eye.

Racial Divides

Racial division in jails varies from country to country, state to state and even prison to prison. In some prisons, race is of little consequence. In others, racial segregation, imposed by either the authorities or enforced unofficially by the prison population, is an issue of major significance.

The jails I served time in were not defined by race. Although there was occasionally tension between different ethnic groups, it was sporadic and largely inconsequential. It seemed to me the acquisition and taking of illicit drugs transcended racial tension, if there was any to begin with. However, from many of the US-based prison documentaries I have seen, it would certainly appear that race is a significant, ongoing issue of concern. Obviously, having only served time in Australia, I cannot offer any inside advice. All I can think to say would be this: if you are going to a prison where race is an issue, apply the mantra – watch, listen and learn. Take the lead from more experienced inmates of your own ethnicity.

There are three common methods of segregation:

- Some prisons will segregate inmates from different cultural backgrounds, so they will have units for different ethnicities to minimise racial tension.
- Some prisons are 'pseudo-segregated' – that is, there is no official policy as such, but inmates are generally placed with people of the same background.
- Some prisons are segregated, but only in the sense the inmates *choose* to segregate themselves. They will share units with other ethnic groups, but interaction between the different groups is minimal.

There is also a fourth kind – jails where race isn't a big issue. There might be sporadic racial tension, but it's rare and usually stems from inmates with a chip on their shoulder. More relevant is how *you* respond to issues of race. If you have strong feelings against another race, *keep it to yourself.* Even if you are talking to someone you think you can trust, be careful – once you have made a racist comment it can't be unsaid. The same logic applies to talking about racial equality. If this is an issue of interest to you, use jail as an educational tool – watch, listen and learn. *But don't preach about it.* You may find some of the talk about other races distasteful, but, once again, keep it to yourself.

The jails I was in (in Australia) were, for the most part, race issue-free. I say for the most part because, although there are some racial divides, they are very, very minimal. I heard people talk about a certain amount of racial segregation in jails in other parts of the country. The stories differed, mainly in the sense that some people talked about actual segregation occurring (the first type I mentioned – jail policy segregation), while others talked about how, although there was no official policy, tensions had risen to the point where the senior management simply found it easier to put people from the same ethnic background in the same units (the second type).

I have been in units that are a bit more like the third type, and these units were mostly in the reception jail – a facility with rude screws, more violence and a transient prison population. Naturally, people with similar cultural backgrounds are going to have things in common, so there's an intrinsic magnetism between these inmates. But it wasn't like Caucasians couldn't be friends with Aboriginals or Africans or Vietnamese or Middle Eastern inmates. People simply found it easier not to make race an issue.

It's always puzzled me why American jails seem so racially divided. It's odd. Everyone is doing time, everyone misses their people and everyone gets locked in a cell at night. No one racial group has it easier in terms of how the rules apply. So why create unnecessary complications? Anyway...

Where I was, race was rarely an issue, let alone a significant one. If an inmate was stupid enough to be blatant about their racist views, then there would be swift repercussions. But I only saw that once, and everyone in the unit saw that one coming. Except, of course, the racist.

TVs and Movies

Not all prisons allow TVs in cells, but there's a good chance you can watch one in a communal setting. TV can be a great distraction. It can also be the cause of tension. People like to watch different things, they have preferences regarding volume and they respond differently to what's being aired, so here's a list of *don'ts* when it comes to TV:

- If you have a TV your own cell, don't have the volume up loud, especially late at night. Other inmates will figure out where it's coming from and it could cause trouble. If need be, simply sit close to the TV with the volume low. With the communal TV, keep the volume low during quiet times (like post-lunch).
- Don't damage the TV – if you damage the communal TV, regardless of whether inmates have a TV in their cells, there's likely to be trouble unless there is some very good explanation. If the communal TV is the *only* TV, explanations, reasonable or not, won't do much good. You will get hurt. If the one in your cell is damaged when you arrive, ask the COs for a replacement. If *you* damage the TV, they will deduct the cost of a replacement (at cost price) from your prison account.
- Don't yell and cheer at top volume during a sporting match on the TV unless everyone else is watching the same thing and behaving the same way (like during a football final). This applies to both personal and communal TV watching.
- *Don't try to light a cigarette using the TV.* This sounds bizarre, but it can be done. The problem is, unless you have been taught (and taught well) by another inmate how

to do this, you risk blowing the fuse in your cell – *plus* the surrounding cells. Come morning, you will have several angry inmates to answer to. They won't be happy they had to go without power all night because you stuffed up.

- Predatory inmates look for any excuse to give 'weaker' inmates a hard time. If you happen to like movies/shows about the police, don't mention this. This can even extend to legal dramas or anything that can be vaguely tied to depictions of authoritarian behaviour.

The Topic of Children

The above advice is also applicable to any shows that feature children. Child-related offences are treated with an air of hysteria, and if you are in mainstream, it's best to avoid the topic of children altogether *unless* you are talking about your own children or close relatives (nieces or nephews, etc.). Also, ask your people to be careful if they happen to send you magazine articles or newspaper articles (they may be doing this to cater to your SI) – specifically, make sure there are no pictures of children in adverts near the article of interest. They may need to cut carefully so you can enjoy your article and appease the prison population. Also check the reverse side of the article – if there are kids, forget it. This sounds over the top and unnecessarily harsh – and that's because it is. The topic of children in jail – just avoid it. No jokes. No facetious remarks. If a children's show is on the communal TV, change the channel. Do this even if you are reading your book on the seats facing the TV – that's how crazy it gets. There's no logical explanation for this collective hypersensitive attitude, except perhaps to differentiate mainstream from protection as much as possible. Whatever the reason, remain vigilant. One distasteful joke could open Pandora's box.

Because I did all my time in mainstream, I simply don't know how the politics of child-related comments would be received by inmates in protection, but I would imagine it would be largely the same, as not all inmates in protection are child-sex offenders. Earlier in the book I talked about why people end up in protection. This book should be applicable to both mainstream and protection, as jail is jail. They get the same food, and they don't get extra privileges. And, to a large extent, the social side of humans is the same the world over, so I hope this text can help all inmates, mainstream or protection.

Music

In Chapter 11, how to obtain CDs and a device to play them on is explained. Music can be a welcome distraction for the inmate with ASD, so having your own stereo or discman and a collection of CDs may help you unwind. If you are listening to music in your cell without headphones, keep the volume low. There will probably be a stereo that gets brought out into the yard for people to listen to music while they exercise. This stereo will belong to an inmate, *not* the jail, so treat it with respect. Some jails have public phones in the yard. Some jails will have them inside. Some jails have both. A blaring stereo can interfere with a phone call, and if it's a much-needed call to one of your people, this is likely to annoy you. Regardless, it's important to demonstrate good prison etiquette.

Don't even touch the stereo at first. As time goes on, and you become a more familiar face in the unit, you can begin asking whether you may turn the stereo down (but not *all* the way down) for a phone call. This will be received well, as other inmates make calls and understand your predicament. Just be polite.

Don't just waltz up and turn it down, even if you see other inmates do this. They will be 'allowed' to do it due to their standing in the social hierarchy. As time goes on, you too will 'earn the right' to lower the volume for your call.

Cell Radios

It's relatively common for jail cells to be equipped with a radio. Not all jails will have this facility, and don't get too excited – it's a very basic device built into the wall. Most inmates don't use them. But some do, and they may fall asleep while listening. The problem with this is the design of the cells – they build them so the plumbing and electrics are back to back, so two cells essentially 'share' the same radio (in the sense that one double-sided radio sits in between the two cells). Therefore, the cell next door may be affected by the sound of the radio. It might not be noticeable while the night is young and you're watching TV, or listening to your side of the radio, but if it's 2.00 am and you can hear the tinny, muffled sound of your *neighbour's* radio, it's very noticeable. Enough to keep you awake. So be sure to avoid antagonising your neighbour by always turning your radio all the way down. If the reverse is happening, and they're doing this to you, politely explain to them the effect it's having on your sleep. They're the one in the wrong, and they know it.

Telephones

Aside from not dominating usage of the phone(s), there are other factors to consider. For example, if a phone's receiver is hanging off the hook, this usually means somebody is planning to make a call but had something else to attend to first (like get mail or meds). So, if you find a phone like this, leave it. Wait for another phone to become available and, if the unit has only one phone, wait for five minutes and if nothing has happened, call out into the yard: 'Is anyone using this phone?' Basically, establish if the phone was off the hook by accident or for a reason. You shouldn't need the skills of Sherlock Holmes to solve the mystery.

While speaking on the phone, keep your voice low (but not so low it looks suspicious), and try to avoid talking about:

- police
- other inmates
- COs
- your dislike of the unit.

During 'rush hour' on the phones (usually between 3.30 pm and 5.00 pm) there may be a 'line-up' to use them. If this is the case, there are usually inmates milling around the vicinity of the phones. Ask if there's a line-up, find out who's last, and say to them, 'I'll go after you then, yeah?' They will either indicate someone else is after them, or they'll confirm they understand you're due to go after them. This process may seem needlessly regimented, but it's because all inmates value talking to their people, and family/friends can usually be reached more easily in the afternoon, after work/school.

Personal Hygiene

Personal hygiene can be an issue for people with ASD. Ensure a basic level of hygiene is maintained. No one will expect you to pluck your eyebrows or style your hair, but they don't want to sit next to someone who hasn't showered for several days.

This is particularly relevant in jail, as inmates (mostly through boredom) maintain high levels of hygiene, to the point where it borders on obsessive. This may seem almost contradictory in a male prison, as jail has very masculine/rough connotations, and preening oneself isn't generally considered masculine, but in jail many inmates shave their legs, their arms and their chest/stomach. *Don't make a comment that could be interpreted by others as suggesting they are somehow feminine or even homosexual to engage in this practice.* Remember, watch, listen and learn. Basically, try to be the good house guest. That way you minimise the chances of a minor issue festering into a big one.

Along with basic hygiene come bodily functions. Now, farts can be funny. Most people will, at some stage in their lives, have giggled or laughed at a fart joke, or a fart in a quiet movie theatre and so on. In jail, it's the same. However, when and where you fart can be an issue. *Don't fart (or burp) at your table while eating, and don't fart deliberately near someone for amusement.* They may not be so amused.

Also, it's considered bad form to use the communal unit toilet to defecate. You will have to hold it in until the next unlock. If you really, really must go, you could risk it, and hope nobody uses the toilet soon after you. This is unlikely to be an issue, as your body will adapt to its new regime, and your bowel movements will begin to sync with access times.

First Names First

Although you may only know another inmate by their last name, avoid calling them by that. The reason: COs will always call out the last name of the prisoner they need to see or are ticking off during headcount. Inmates avoid doing this to distance themselves from COs. If you call someone by their surname, they may take issue with it and cause trouble. Stick to first names, nicknames or 'mate', 'buddy', etc.

Long Showers

A common way for people to relax is with a hot shower. If you are doubled-up (sharing a cell), don't have overly long showers because your cellmate might be trying to listen to a show or the radio, or trying to sleep. Some jails have a different type of plumbing system to a house or unit complex, and showering can make a loud 'chug chug chug' sound, which the whole unit can hear. People don't mind this provided:

- the shower is 15 minutes or less
- showers are *not* taken after 10.00 pm or before 5.00 am.

One of the stranger things that I encountered during my incarceration was an inmate who was flushing his toilet all night long (at least it felt like that), and in the morning the screws went to check on him because he didn't emerge from his cell after unlock. It turned out he was in there, completely naked, after having spent the previous evening methodically tearing up, then flushing, all his clothes. They took him away after that, and I don't know what became of him.

CHAPTER 13

Sharing a Cell

Introduction

At the end of the last chapter showering etiquette when doubled-up was mentioned. Because there is more to social etiquette than having short showers when doubled-up, a portion of this book is specifically devoted to helping the inmate with ASD understand what to expect when sharing a cell. This includes practicalities, basic behavioural expectations, potential areas of conflict (and how to deal with them) and techniques to help you cope with living in such close quarters with another inmate. This chapter won't be able to address *all* the issues that may come to the fore while sharing a cell, largely because how you fare will depend on your and your cellmate's idiosyncrasies. These two sets of variables make it difficult to offer much more than basic, tentative advice.

As mentioned throughout the book, your diagnosis is a genuine reason to request a single cell, and you may in fact get one either straight away or very quickly. Therefore, some of this advice might be moot. However, it is included because although you will have a strong case for a single cell, nothing in life is guaranteed and you may well find yourself sharing a cell, at least initially. Plus, you may not want to share your diagnosis, as discussed in Chapter 5.

Practicalities

First, it's important to distinguish between 'official' double-up cells and the ethically dubious practice of squashing two adults into a cell built for one. Prisons don't like doing the latter, as it leads to the sort of tension one would expect – increased fighting between inmates *and* increased assaults on COs. Overcrowding is an issue that doesn't attract the resources it so sorely needs because of political reasons – either the current government is 'cracking down on crime' (political speak for targeting minor crime, like drug possession and the like) or it's a 'budget issue' (the government can find the money to build sporting stadiums but not desperately needed jails).

If you end up with a cellmate (cellie), but the cell is built for one, don't worry about having to sleep on the floor, it won't be for long. If two of you are assigned the same cell at the same time (unlikely), you will just have to negotiate who ends up on the floor. If you are assigned to a cell with someone already in it (likely), you will be on the floor. When your cellie leaves, it's your 'right' to take over the bed, and the 'new guy' sleeps on the floor.

If you end up in a cell designed for two, it will make life easier. These 'double-up' cells are bigger, have bunkbeds (the bottom one is considered preferable), and have two sets of shelves for you and your cellie's wares. As mentioned before, there is usually a camera in designated double-up cells, so keep this in mind if you plan to breach the rules (e.g. by smoking).

As for the toilet, it may be a new and very uncomfortable experience having to defecate with someone else literally two metres away. But (no pun intended) you will adapt. When your cellie is doing his business, lean back and look away. Pretend you're not there. When you're using the toilet, remember to give a 'courtesy flush' as soon as your stool is out, so it minimises the odour of faeces. Once you've cleaned your buttocks, flush again. If you have left behind a sample of your wares on the inside of the bowl, be sure to scrub it off with the toilet brush. *Defecating in such close quarters with someone will be challenging at first, but you will get used to it. Everybody does. The need for the human body to evacuate its bowels will eventually override any cognitive reluctance, regardless of how much the concept bothers you.*

The same practice (of using 'courtesy flushes' and cleaning your faecal matter) applies to flatulence – some people seem to think it's possible to just 'hold it in' every time the urge comes along. As everybody knows, do this too much and you will end up with painful abdominal bloating. The trick when doubled-up is to release wind when your buttocks are firmly encased within your bedding, essentially trapping the odour. While not a perfect method, it's surprisingly effective. The other option is to sit on the toilet and release wind, then do a 'courtesy flush' so the odour is 'sucked' into the drainage system. This might not sound plausible, but the plumbing systems in jails are different – less water, more vacuum. It works well for minimising odour.

Basic Behavioural Expectations

Behaviour inside your cell should be akin to behaviour outside your cell. That is, act like the good house guest and ensure your 'presence' is minimal:

- Always be polite, even if you are grumpy or have had a bad day.
- Listen, and don't dominate the conversation.
- Avoid excessive talk about your SI.
- Don't make assumptions.
- Minimise talk about issues like race, politics or religion, at least until you know your cellie's stance.
- Don't complain about another inmate's behaviour to your cellie – it just might make it back to them (and vice versa: don't complain to another inmate about your cellie).
- Don't talk about the COs in a way that could be construed as 'being on their side'.
- If your cellie chooses to use drugs, don't make it an issue. Just act like it's not happening, and don't tell other inmates about what your cellie gets up to – it's their private business, not yours to use as a conversation starter.
- Be careful about making racist/sexist/distasteful jokes – you can never be sure what someone's 'hot-button' issue might be.
- Don't steal, even so much as a piece of chocolate. It's bad form, and you wouldn't want it happening to you.

Aside from these specific examples, use your common sense. If you find you and your cellie frequently disagree about things, perhaps consider requesting a change of cell. 'Cabin fever' can set in quickly if you are regularly at odds with your cellmate.

Masturbation

Most men, both behind the razor wire and on the other side, will engage in masturbation as a form of relaxation, self-pleasure and a highly effective (albeit short) distraction from the world around you. If you have your own cell, feel free to indulge yourself – just remember to begin masturbating straight *after* the COs have done their regular night rounds, so you get a good two-hour window to relax and enjoy yourself. Having a torch flashed in your face is not conducive to a state of arousal. As for masturbating while doubled-up, the best bet is to wait until you can hear your cellie emitting sounds that suggest they are well and truly asleep, like snoring, lack of tossing and turning, slow, steady breathing and even sleep talk/mumbling. Just be sure to keep the noise to a minimum and clean up any mess left behind. Also, having ASD can manifest in a lack of tact. In relation to masturbation, the social protocol is to keep the news to yourself. You can join in the banter about 'jerking off' when it's discussed in the yard and such, but what your cellie *doesn't* need to hear upon waking is: 'Bro, you should have seen the load I shot last night. It must have been building up – it practically hit me in the face!'

Potential Areas of Conflict

During my time inside, I was doubled-up with five different people, all with quite different personalities. The duration of time spent doubled-up varied – one inmate was there for only a night, while the longest one was three months. I was doubled-up in cells designed for one and doubled-up in cells designed for two. I'm basing this part of the chapter on what I observed as common, recurring areas of conflict, along with what I heard fellow inmates gripe about when they discussed being 'doubled-up'.

The TV

One TV, two inmates. This isn't conducive to harmony. However, if you land a reasonable cellmate, you will be able negotiate what to watch. If your cellmate *seems* not to care, still check that what you are watching is okay with them. If *you* really don't care what's on, say so. If you do care, and there are particular shows you really enjoy watching, ask in advance if it's okay to 'book' the TV for your favourite show. That way, it won't come out of the blue. Hopefully, your cellie will extend the same courtesy to you. If your cellie seems intent on being the alpha male and dictating what you watch every night, consider asking for a different cellmate. It's likely their 'channel hogging' is the thin end of the wedge, and if you stay paired up with them, they will begin telling you when you can shower, what time you should wake up and so on.

Lights out

Different people have different sleeping patterns, so this must be considered when sharing a cell. The designated double-up cells have the lights arranged so you can be on either bunk and have enough light to read while not disturbing your cellie. If you're squashed into a single cell, it's a bit more difficult. The best suggestion is to buy a small reading light on STP buy-up (see Chapter 11), so you can read into the night without it becoming a source of conflict. People with ASD often have sleeping difficulties, so this could be a sage investment.

If your cellie likes to watch TV into the wee hours, don't stress – you will probably find yourself adapting. If you don't adapt, request a change of cellmate. If you want to watch all night, ask your cellie if this bothers them. If it does, reach a compromise as to when the TV goes off.

Showering

If you are in a jail that has timed showers, be sure *not to use all the hot water before your cellie has a chance to get clean*. This doesn't mean you have to shower together; rather you get out when the first four-minute cycle has stopped. They will be set to run two cycles in the morning and night, both in designated double-up cells *and* when there's two inmates sharing a single cell.

If the showers are not timed, don't have a 20-minute shower, even if it feels really good. It's okay now and again, just don't make a habit of it.

One of my cellmates would regularly stand in the shower for about 25–30 minutes. It was because he was shaving his chest, arms and legs. I thought it was odd, because he didn't work out, and it's usually the inmates with buff bodies who like to preen themselves. He was a good guy, but it started to wear thin after a few weeks of it. The cell would steam up to the point where I couldn't see the TV from 1.5 metres away, I would start to sweat and things would get damp. It was obnoxious. I put up and shut up, not because I was scared, but because I was new and didn't want to make waves. But, as you can see from this anecdote, showers can cause friction between cellmates.

General cleanliness

In line with the 'good house guest' ethos comes general tidiness. It may surprise you how quickly a cell can look dishevelled despite inmates not actually being in possession of many items. On the outside, it's nice to come home to a clean and tidy house. On the inside, it's nice to come 'home' to a clean and tidy cell. The older and/or more seasoned your cellie, the more important this becomes. Put your rubbish in the bin. If you throw your apple core at the bin and miss, pick it up and put it in there. If you spill some of your drink, wipe it up. It's not rocket science. Think of it as if you are constantly being 'graded' on your cleanliness (which, in a way, you are).

Also, remember to pull your weight when it comes to 'inspection day' (see Chapter 11).

In the first-timers unit, the same guy who took excessively long showers would also magically 'disappear' (as much as one can in a confined space like a jail unit) whenever we were due to clean our cell. I would find him cutting laps in the yard or playing a sneaky hand of cards. It didn't bother me too much (again because I was new). In hindsight, however, I realised I was practising good form – the sort that would put me in good stead when it came to being clean and responsible in placement jail, where things were tougher and repercussions swifter and more severe. I don't know whether my cellie ever went to placement jail (his crime was relatively minor), but if he tried that bullshit there, it would go down like the proverbial lead balloon.

Ideological clashes

When you have been in the same cell with someone for a few weeks, then a couple of months, you start to see the deeper, less superficial side of them. They take off their prison 'mask', and sometimes what you see is not pretty. You may find they are overtly homophobic, racist, misogynistic or cruel. This may not bother you at first, but people with ASD have their own set of ideological values, and if they are at odds with your cellie's, it will eventually become a rub, which becomes a sore, which can become a wound. Unfortunately, the only treatment is to find a new cellmate. Neither of you is going to change such intrinsic beliefs, so it's best to agree to disagree and go your separate ways. By the time these opinions are voiced, it may well be time for a change anyway.

Soothing Techniques

Chapter 17 examines psychological techniques applicable to your entire jail experience, and as such is also relevant to being doubled-up. However, this portion of the chapter provides tips specific to easing the stress of sharing a cell:

- Avoid your cellie during the day – not in a rude way by any means, but you'll appreciate the space after the novelty of living with them has worn off.
- If you really crave some 'downtime', try to negotiate with your cellie if one of the access times can be 'yours'. This way you can lie on a soft bed, with no interruptions, even if just for a couple of hours.
- If you have a stereo with headphones, or a discman, listen to music while your cellie is watching TV. You can escape into your own 'bubble' this way.
- The same goes for reading. You may be surprised how easy it is to tune out the sound of the TV if you have a really good book. Immerse yourself in the world of fiction (or non-fiction, as the case may be).
- Talk to your people on the phone, or via mail, about your frustrations. Just be sure to keep your voice nice and low. Offloading frustrations to those who know you well and care for you is probably the most effective technique of all.

- Remember, you can always move. The authorities aren't likely to make you stay in a cell with someone if you insinuate it could end in violence.
- Finally, if your cellie is really getting to you, try looking at them with a sense of compassion. This may sound difficult, but if done successfully, instead of feeling anger and despair, you'll end up feeling distanced and calm.

The cellie I stayed the longest with, about two months, seemed like a good guy at first: educated, very intelligent and with a decent sense of humour. There was just one problem – he was an alpha male through and through. When he realised, after a few days, that I was able to verbally joust with him at his level, he started getting difficult. He dominated the TV, demanded I stay quiet at certain times, but would get up at 2.00 am, turn on the main light and make a coffee, before putting on the TV. If I did that, he would be livid. He was the consummate hypocrite. By the time I asked to be moved, I wanted to strangle him. The point is, no matter how patient you are, everybody has their breaking point. Make sure you request movement before either one of you reaches yours.

Finally

As mentioned before, this is an important chapter to include, because being 'doubled-up' is a very real possibility, even if you do tell the authorities about your ASD. It's likely you will be allocated your own cell, but this may not happen quickly. In the meantime, try to remember what you read here, and know that inmates with ASD have come and gone before you and coped.

CHAPTER 14

Social Interaction
with Other Inmates

Introduction

Some people instinctively identify those who are 'different', including those with ASD. The thoughtful, kind person will try to help the 'outcast' feel welcome. The social predator will view the 'outcast' as a target – a person to make fun of, somebody to taunt for a few cheap laughs. Worse still, the 'outcast' may become the victim of systematic bullying. Many individuals with ASD will have experienced bullying during school or in workplaces, and although this means the victim understands exactly what's happening, it does little to cushion the psychological blows of victimisation.

This chapter looks at some of the more common situations where antisocial behaviour may present itself and gives general advice on how to minimise the chances of having to deal with antagonistic inmates.

Prison Politics

Behind bars, there is a term used by inmates to describe gossip or rumours circulating between inmates. This term is 'politics'. For example, you may see an inmate with a black eye, and if you were to ask someone what happened, their response may simply be: 'Ahh, it's nothing. Just politics.'

Please note
The example given above is based on a theoretical exchange between you and an inmate you know and trust. *Do not go around asking about an inmate's injuries – it is essentially none of your business.*

Remember the adage: See no evil, hear no evil, speak no evil. If you see something that breaches prison rules, pretend you *didn't* see it. If you hear something salacious, keep it to yourself (this includes not telling other inmates), and speak no evil – don't tell on people, and don't criticise people behind their backs.

The inmate with ASD should stay as far away from prison politics as possible. But don't keep your head buried in the sand – it's helpful to have a *general* sense of what's going on. Put simply: be aware, but not involved.

A Trying Time

Annoyingly, regardless of what you say or do, some inmates will find it irresistible to make your life difficult. They do this for a few reasons:

- boredom
- status among other inmates
- they are bullies at heart
- they have a 'better him than me' attitude
- they're weak
- they're unhappy.

Irrespective of their motives, the outcome is the same – inmates who are different are singled out. Some units are worse than others when it comes to bullying or harassment. It's a gamble, a concept people with ASD find uncomfortable. We want to control our environments to the point where (for some) every day and activity is micromanaged. You must (temporarily) leave this way of life at the gates – although you can micromanage *some* facets of prison life (like the way your cell is arranged, what you get on buy-up or what exercise you choose to do), there are many you can't. Focus on watching, listening and figuring out who's who. But remember, be as subtle as possible about this.

As mentioned before, if life in a regular unit becomes too much to handle, there is always the option of applying for the SNU, using your diagnosis as leverage. If you are looking at a longer stretch behind bars (three or more years), doing it in a unit free of low-level (but relentless) heckling may be the difference between coping and having a breakdown.

For a more thorough look at the SNU and whether it appeals to you, see Chapter 5.

Buy-ups and Standover 'Men'

In Chapter 11, prison 'buy-ups' (or visiting the 'canteen') were explained. What wasn't discussed is the risk new or victimised inmates face when it comes to their purchases. The single most helpful piece of advice is this: when new to jail, or even you have moved to a new unit, *start with small buy-ups*. That way other inmates can't logically accuse you of having enough money to buy them things, or part with them once bought. Over time you will feel more at ease in the unit and can begin buying more. If you have assimilated relatively well, it won't even be noticed.

How Standover 'Men' Operate

Harassment may start on the day buy-up forms are due, with inmates either overtly or subtly attempting to coerce you into buying them items. The easiest way to circumvent this is to simply say, 'I don't have the money. Sorry.' There's no way this inmate can know the state of your finances – COs are very careful to ensure account balances are kept private. When buy-up arrives, they may try coercing you into handing over some of your items. Watch out for inmates who say, 'So, what'd you get mate?' and then proceed to enter your personal space to either peer into your bags or, worse, start rifling through them. If this happens, say as jovially as possible, 'Come on, get out of it!' and try to reassert your right *not* to have your personal space invaded. Making physical contact may be necessary to do this, in the sense of using your body to shield your goods, or essentially 'push' the inmate away. This may feel foreign, and elicit anxious or fearful feelings, but remember: *this moron is not minding his business, he's trying to make you feel scared, and that is not okay.* Being assertive from day dot is a major factor in minimising the risk of victimisation.

Sometimes inmates who are into the drug scene will ask if you are interested in a swap. There are two reasons this is a bad idea:

- Doing drugs in jail is really stupid.
- The inmate won't fulfil his end of the bargain.

Getting the Goods into Your Cell

COs don't want people sitting around getting agitated because they must guard their buy-ups from light-fingered inmates, so they will either organise the buy-ups to arrive near access time, or they will allow a brief access to put your buy-up away. If there is a delay, stay by your goods.

I was fortunate in the sense I experienced no problems with buy-ups, even though sometimes what I was buying would create the illusion I had bought loads of stuff. This was due to large amounts of noodles, cereal and crackers being bought. They all took up a lot of room. By the time I was almost due for full-time release, I knew my buy-up to the letter. It was all health food by then, because of my pseudo-obsessional exercising. But I did know one guy, a kid really, who had trouble with his buy-up. He had come across from the boy's yard (not quite juvenile detention, not quite adult jail) when he turned 18. He was nice, mild-mannered. Not the brightest bulb in the chandelier but not a fool. I picked him as adapting to life behind bars with relative ease. Wrong. He was quickly befriended by an older, seasoned inmate. This inmate was wiry, tense – like a giant spring compressed with frayed rubber bands. He convinced this poor kid that, once they got to the 'big bad placement jail', he would need help. He would need 'protection'. And who better for the job than the one scaring the kid in the first place?

I found all this out months later, from a reliable source. This piece-of-shit bully was getting the kid to buy him all and sundry from the buy-up list. His whole buy-up was going to this so-called man. It was times like that I wish I was proficient in some form of martial art, and could have, well, rectified the problem myself, had I run into the bully on the walkway. Luckily the kid got out, and has, as far as I know, stayed out. I don't know or care about the bully. Hopefully karma got him in the end.

Gambling

While technically against jail policy, gambling is rarely met with punishment. COs turn a blind eye to gambling, provided the inmates keep it largely covered from the camera's ever-roaming eye, and it doesn't cause an unacceptable level of friction between inmates. To the inmate with ASD: *don't get involved in gambling.* Even if you have a remarkable affinity for cards, and are confident you could make a few dollars, this isn't like a Saturday-night poker game with friends. Put simply, inmates won't always play fair. It's a jail, and running an honest operation doesn't exactly come naturally. They can work together to fleece you and, without going into needless detail of how they do this, ask yourself: is it worth it? A debt can spiral with interest, and a problem gambler will simply keep on playing in a vain attempt to win back his losses. Violence will follow an unpaid debt, and, in a worst-case scenario, drive an inmate into protection, or if they're *already* in protection, into solitary confinement. You can play cards without gambling.

Working Out

Exercise is one of the most effective ways for the inmate with ASD to relax – it gets those feel-good chemicals flowing.

Exercise etiquette is more important than you might think. Try following these guidelines:

- Exercise can form part of an inmate's daily routine, so interrupting *while* they're in 'the zone' can throw them off their rhythm. Not a good thing.
- If an inmate criticises your technique, take it on board and thank them. Even if they're wrong, there's no harm done.
- Always ask if an inmate has finished in an area of the yard with exercise equipment (like the dip bars), even if they aren't physically in that space anymore. They may be taking a breather. The thoughtful inmate (you!) will put a towel or shirt or drink or *something* down to indicate the area is being used.
- Wipe down sweat, and if you happen to be in a smoking jail, make sure you don't sit there with a smoke, letting it waft into the faces of people exercising.
- If an inmate is doing an exercise using an overtly incorrect technique, you can tell them. Just introduce yourself, be friendly and explain you are trying to stop them injuring themselves. If their technique for an exercise is only a little off, don't bother correcting them. You will appear to be a know-it-all.
- If inmates are working out together, and they *always* work out together, expect them to be a bit selfish in sharing equipment. It's best to either find an alternative exercise for that body part or forget it and do it later. If the group get an inkling you want to use a part of the yard, they will probably go out of their way to be obstructive.
- Don't say annoying/unhelpful things like 'Run, Forrest, run!' to people jogging, or yell 'Adrian!' (as in *Rocky*) to people working the pads (boxing). Basically, unless you exercise yourself, don't provide commentary to people who do.

Perhaps they really do have a nicely stocked rack of free weights in American jails, as seen in the movies, but they don't in Australia. Well, at least not in any jails I served time in. So, when it comes to working out, inmates become inventive. Most muscle groups can be worked on using calisthenics, but isolating and exercising the biceps can be a bit tricky.

At one jail, we would wait until the screws were distracted, then quickly grab two industrial-strength buckets and fill them with water. Those buckets were great – wrap a t-shirt around the handle, and there you have it – weighted bicep curls.

At the placement jail, they kept those buckets locked up – I guess for that very reason. So in lieu of buckets, we would sneak our washing bags out, put two medicine balls in there for weight and it would have the same effect.

One day, this screw saw me and warned me not to use washing bags for anything other than washing. Being the stubborn Aspie I am, I simply asked my buddies to block the view. But the screw saw me (again), and he was livid. He came charging out into the yard: 'What did I just tell you? Just two minutes ago! Blah blah blah...'

He called me inside, went into the fish bowl (the nickname we used for the screws' office) and said, 'Right, you can either go get the medicine balls and bring them to me right now, or I'll breach you.'

'Chief,' I said calmly, 'I can't do that.'

'What? What do you mean you can't do that?' he practically spat at me.

'Because,' I explained, 'if I go out there and obey a direct order from a CO, I will become a potential target for other inmates.'

Then it got sort of strange. The screw started mouthing off to me, not loudly, but in a very crude and inappropriate manner.

'Oh,' he said in a mock tone of concern. 'Are you scared of having cocks in your virgin arsehole?'

211

I did a double take. I couldn't believe he'd just said that. I think the other screw was taken aback too, judging by the look on this face.

'Are you worried about having five men pump you up the bum? Is that what you're saying?'

I was speechless (extremely rare for me).

Then the other screw stepped in, saying something to me like 'Look, just fill in this form, the senior manager will look at it, and we go from there.'

As I took the form, the aggressive screw was making sucking noises and kiss-kiss faces. The normal screw looked embarrassed.

When I was hauled before the senior management, the head honcho looked at the breach, asked me what had happened, then examined the paper to see who had submitted the breach. As soon as he saw the name, he paused, sighed, rolled his eyes and shot a knowing glance at a colleague. Then he said to me, 'Mr Attwood, in future, please follow instructions given to you by staff. As for this,' he wiggled the paper, 'consider it a warning. Dismissed.'

I guess the screw wasn't very popular among the staff either.

Table Etiquette

Initially, when new to a unit, you're going to be asking yourself, 'Where do I sit?' and 'What's the protocol for meal times?' Basically, you line up, get your food, see a spot that looks 'right' for you (inmates of a similar age, or inmates you have noticed reading a bit or spending a fair amount of time alone) and ask if you can sit with them. Because it's early days, and nobody has had the time to form an opinion about you (justified or otherwise), they have no reason to say no. *If* they give you the cold shoulder, don't overthink it. Just try another table. Those inmates are probably people you don't want to know anyway.

Obviously, basic table manners apply, and it should either be a group effort to clean the table after the meal, or there should be a rotating system. If some smartarse has picked you as being different, as someone who *doesn't* want to settle problems using violence, they may start a negative pattern by simply expecting you to do their share of the work. This behaviour needs to be nipped in the bud, before it becomes an issue. The other inmate may threaten violence. If they do, stand your ground. This will be difficult. For most people with ASD, physical confrontation is something avoided at all costs. However, asserting yourself will earn you respect, even if there *is* violence. It might sound scary (and it can be) but remember: it's a matter of short-term pain, long-term gain. As for table etiquette, it's straightforward:

- Act like the adult you are.
- Use manners.
- Don't feel obliged to make small talk.
- Avoid talking about other inmates.
- Keep the discussion light.
- Do your share to keep your communal table clean.

And do not try to steal any food! If you find the meals aren't making you feel full, you can do things like get tokens on buy-up (see Chapter 11) and see if anyone you know wants to swap their dinner for a couple of tokens. You may be surprised how many inmates would rather get a can or two of soft drink (soda) than eat their dinner.

What if you want to eat alone? This might be your preference, especially if you need somewhere relatively calm compared with the loud, echo-prone unit. There are two options for this:

1. You *can* choose to eat outside and, if you feel confident, you can start doing this the first night you're there. Otherwise, you can start off with small steps that get increasingly bigger. For example, during lunch, make your sandwich at the table, clean up your mess, then take it into the yard to eat. After a while you can start to eat your dinner in the calm of the yard.

2. You can take your lunch sandwich into your cell to eat during afternoon access, and/or you can take your dinner into your cell. Many inmates practise this at night, as they enjoy eating while watching TV, or they prefer to eat their dinner at a later hour than 4.30 pm.

Please note

Some jails will have a policy that states meals are to be eaten at the tables only. If this is the case, don't break the rules – some smart-alec CO might just decide to impose a 'collective punishment' and lock down the whole unit. While unlikely, it's well within the realms of possibility. You don't want to be the one responsible for a 'collective punishment'. If you want to eat outside but don't know if you're allowed to, just watch – if the COs are cool with you eating outside, you will see other inmates doing this. *Don't just ask a fellow inmate – they could lie just to get you in trouble.*

Visits

In Chapter 11, the *practical* side of visits was explained: how to arrange them, how non-contact visits work and so on. This segment will look at the social side of visits – that is, the social side of the whole visitation process, not just the fact you will be seeing your visitors. The first point to emphasise is that visits are one of a handful of situations during which inmates from units across the jail can meet and interact. The other situations are a chance run-in at medical, during a class or passing each other by coincidence on the walkways. This is important to remember because if you have accidently stood on the wrong inmate's toes (but haven't stressed about it for a while because you and he moved units after your run-in), remember *you just might see this individual down at visits* and this is not good. Granted, the odds are slim, but you should put some thought into whether you consider the visit worth the risk of confrontation.

During my final ten months behind bars in placement jail, I spent most of them in the SNU, primarily because of my ASD, but also because I had managed to get some inmates off side and saw residing in the SNU as a very good idea. Were there issues of pride? Asking to be moved to a unit known to be 'soft'? Sure, but after I saw just how comparatively great the SNU was, I didn't give a shit. I had spent enough time in units full of bullies and wannabe gangsters, and made a conscious and informed decision to remove myself from them. That way, I did all my time in mainstream, but didn't have to worry about all the alpha male bullshit that goes on in many units. Although I missed my family, I wasn't prepared to risk running into one of my 'enemies' during a visit. I could talk to my people on the phone, which was enough. We also sent letters to each other. Basically, I could 'socialise' with my family and friends, but not worry about visits and subsequently running into someone big and scary and angry. And I know fights happened at visits (not in the actual visiting area, but in the holding cells inmates wait in prior to being searched before going back to their units).

215

On more than one occasion, while going down to medical to get my testosterone, I could see screws cleaning up after a fight that had happened at visits. They would use a lot of bleach, so now the smell of bleach reminds me of placement jail.

Other Things to Remember About Visits

Naturally, not everyone with ASD will have stood on any toes, and many of you will rightly look forward to being able to see your family. Obviously, if you are in protection, you go to visits with other inmates who are also in protection. It also pays to remember:

- Drugs come in through visits, so you may be warned to not be too intimate with your girlfriend/boyfriend.
- *No one can go to the toilet during visits, even children.* This is to stop drug transactions. So, if you have a weak bladder, factor that in (the same applies to those visiting you).
- Don't pay much attention to other inmates and who's visiting them. Some inmates are paranoid, and a slightly prolonged gaze might be enough for them to become confrontational after the visit is over.
- Legal visits are at a different time and day to family/friend visiting days, and you will be warned well in advance if your legal team is coming to see you. If you have run afoul of any inmates, don't skip the legal visit. Because lawyers only see inmates occasionally, the odds of you running into an 'enemy' is very, very slim.

Finally, when you're waiting with the other inmates to head into or leave the visiting area, remember – see no evil, hear no evil, speak no evil.

Respecting the Unit and the People in It

For seasoned inmates, jail is like a home away from home. For lifers, jail *is* their home. Applying this information to various situations will put you in good stead. As said before, act like a guest in someone's house. If you were making a cup of tea on your friend's benchtop, and you spilled some, you'd clean it up. The same logic applies in jail. If you abide by this code of courtesy, you will appear confident, and if you display good manners and pull your weight when it comes to keeping yourself and your surroundings clean and tidy, you will minimise the risk of inadvertently rubbing someone up the wrong way (including the COs). Here are some examples of abiding by this code:

- Don't assume that because another inmate has a job as kitchen worker, it's *their* responsibility to tidy up after other inmates. They have other responsibilities – ones more pressing than continually wiping down the kitchen bench after messy inmates.
- Apply this logic to all the unit workers. If, for example, you are doing some washing on a Sunday (the day usually designated for neither the top nor the bottom landing, but rather for anyone to use), make sure you leave the laundry as clean as you found it.
- If you see something that needs to be tidied up (like there's some rubbish on the ground around the bin), tidy it. Other inmates may not notice at first, but they soon will. It's a good thing to have a reputation as an inmate who's prepared to go out of their way for the communal good of the unit.
- When in the yard, *don't* just throw your apple core or banana peel over the fence. It will be another inmate who cleans it up – not the COs. There is almost always a bin in the yard – use it.

- If you have a game of cards or Scrabble, try to have it at your designated table. If another inmate from your table is already using that space, *ask before you set up a game at another table*. And, of course, tidy up when you have finished!
- *Never* go through somebody's belongings (the items they bring out for the day, which sit near their cells or under their table) without the express permission of that inmate.
- Avoid sitting on tables or benchtops, or anywhere where food is served or eaten.
- Inmates' clean washing is usually stacked in a place central to the cells. Because the only soft furnishings in the unit are in your cell (the mattress, blanket and pillow) some inmates gravitate towards these bags and use them as pillows. This is fine, *provided the bag of washing belongs to the inmate who's using it.*

The above list of social dos and don'ts could theoretically be massive, and trying to cover everything would be difficult and ultimately pointless. Harness the skills of thinking before you speak/act, remembering your place in the hierarchy, being aware of inmates who are doing long stretches and trying your best to think, 'What repercussions, short and long term, might arise from this social situation?' It sounds complicated, but you will learn quickly. Remember, watch, listen and learn.

When a Fight Breaks Out

Prisons are violent places. There's really no escaping it. Even if you yourself have no intention of picking fights (a good policy to live by), there will still be violence around you. One of the characteristics of many people with ASD is a heightened sensitivity to social and emotional atmosphere. Adapting to prison violence will be one of the more challenging aspects of life behind bars. Tips on dealing with this stress can be found in Chapter 17. This segment addresses how to react if a fight breaks out.

1. *Don't* bring it to the attention of the COs. This may seem obvious, but some inept inmates do it.
2. *Don't* try to break it up. It will either be broken up by COs, the fight will come to a natural end (with both combatants shaking hands to indicate the issue is over) or the winner's friends will pull them off the loser if they are taking it too far.
3. Don't make any comments about the fight. It could make you appear 'interested' in fighting and that can have negative repercussions.
4. Remember, inmates can be quite 'het up' or agitated after a fight, so tread lightly. Not that there is any reason *you personally* would be assaulted, but rather *everyone* is at an elevated risk of confrontation.
5. If you get asked by COs if you saw anything, it's the same protocol as always: see no evil, hear no evil, speak no evil. They won't be expecting you to give them details anyway, so just try to appear blasé and unsure about what happened.
6. Don't go around asking other inmates what the fight was about. It's bad form, and if you really needed to know, you would.

Unless it involves you, stay away from and appear uninterested in fights. This helps you look like someone who isn't easily rattled and doesn't want to get involved in prison politics – and that's the type of inmate who poses no threat, and thus gets left alone (theoretically, at least).

Over time I became very sensitive to the sounds that preceded a fight, to the point I would start if somebody pushed their chair out too fast or squeaked their shoe on the floor – these were sounds that one would often hear just before a fight kicked off. Obviously, there were many false alarms, but like a dog with thunderstorms, I never really got used to it, even when I was moved to the SNU. I really hate violence, but in jail violence is like a dialect: some are proficient in it, some know the basics and others, like me, aren't even interested in trying to speak it. But we could hear it. And I suspect, with my Asperger's, I heard it louder than most. I don't say this to try to alarm anyone reading this book who may be facing time – I say it because it's true, and writing a book that glossed over or lied about the tougher aspects of life behind bars would be insulting and, moreover, useless.

Going Home Etiquette

Ninety-nine per cent of prisoners are grateful to be leaving when their release date comes around or they get granted parole. There are inmates who, like the fictional character Brooks in Stephen King's *The Shawshank Redemption*, don't want to leave. Prison is the only world they know. These inmates are few and far between. It will be difficult not to get excited when your release date draws near, but that doesn't mean you should let your guard down. Here are some recommendations regarding pre-release behaviour:

- Be vague about your release date during your stay behind bars: the less your fellow inmates know about when you're leaving, the less time they have to try to coerce you into smuggling out letters and/or harass you about sending them this and that (money or drugs) once free.

- If you're in a good unit and have friends to talk to about your looming release, don't overdo it. For some inmates, that day is a long, long way away.
- Don't be provocative and carry on about soon having access to things inmates don't. It will make you look childish at best and give you a bloodied lip at worst.
- It's unofficial inmate 'policy' to leave any items you have accumulated to your friends. So, if you bought sneakers, sunglasses, a watch, etc. – leave them to your fellow inmates. It's the way it's been done for years and it looks narrowminded and selfish to walk out to freedom clutching a bag of stuff that is worth next to nothing outside but that could mean a lot to an inmate still locked up.
- Don't promise your things to more than one person. And the rule is this: the first to ask 'Can I have your _____ when you go?' is the one who gets it. If another inmate says they want the item, tell them to talk to the person you have committed to.
- Don't say anything you may have pent up, either to a CO or a fellow inmate. It looks good to leave with dignity, and if you are leaving on parole, remember – you might be back.

It's straightforward: when it's your turn to leave, remember that *you* appreciated it when others didn't rub their upcoming freedom in your face.

Topics to Avoid

Even in the outside world it's important to differentiate between what ought to be kept inside one's head, and what can be vocalised. For people with ASD, on the whole we find this process more challenging than a neurotypical person. On the outside, there is a lot more room for manoeuvre if you make a 'social mistake' – such as simply leaving the party or driving away from a road-rage incident. In jail, you *can't* run away. At least, not in the way you can on the outside. In jail, if you run, and end up requesting to leave a unit because of intimidation, *it will follow you around*. It won't be long before someone in your new unit gets word through the prison grapevine that you 'bailed' from such-and-such a unit, and they will assume you are some sort of 'informer'. Ideally you want to be just another face in the unit. Neither extroverted nor seemingly out of your depth. A big part of 'flying under the radar' is making sure you don't put your foot in your mouth, which is why you need to keep your topic choice in check, at least to begin with. You will hear loudmouth inmates and wonder, 'Why are *they* "allowed" to get away with that?' Well, there could be several reasons:

- They could be in for a long time (so they don't care about stepping on toes).
- They might be on a high rung of the 'drug ladder'.
- They may have powerful connections.
- They may have proved themselves to be very adept at fighting.

But just because other inmates let them 'get away with it', it doesn't mean they actually like the inmate and their behaviour. They just put up with it. As will you. As time goes on, and you feel more settled in your unit, obviously you are entitled to voice your opinion. Having said this, try to avoid commenting on these specific topics:

- Criminal acts you see on the news or read about in the paper (or even listen to on your crappy in-cell radio). Not so much the act itself, but rather how you perceive it. Jail has a strange, slightly warped 'moral code', where some crimes are considered 'worse' than others, with no consistent reasons as to why.

- Whether you think a CO is attractive. While most inmates seem not to care, there are others who believe all COs are bad news. To suggest you are attracted to a CO won't go down well with some inmates.
- Issues of race – you don't know for sure how people feel about other races, so, again, just avoid the topic altogether.
- Speculation out loud as to who you think could beat whom in a fight. If you do this, you risk having one or the other (or some idiot trying to make a name for himself) turning on you: 'If you think so-and-so isn't tough, go and see for yourself.' This could easily escalate into a physical confrontation.
- Don't make value judgements, like suggesting somebody is stupid because they think this or they think that. People with ASD can have intellectual abilities superior to those of their peers and may not suffer fools gladly. *In jail, forget all that. You want to avoid trouble, not prove your intellectual prowess.*

It's a matter of using the old saying: think before you speak. Don't pay lip service to the concept either – inside, one wrong comment can leave you hurt and humiliated. This isn't meant to frighten readers, but it's important to mention it.

Offers of Protection

There are predators in jail. Some want buy-up, some want drugs, some pick fights for no good reason. There are also inmates in jail who dislike the bullies (bullies are, generally, disliked by everyone, including themselves). There are also inmates who are prepared to offer 'protection' in exchange for whatever it is they want, such as:

- tobacco (if it's a smoking jail)
- money (put into an outside account by your people)
- goods on buy-up ($X worth of items per week)
- STP goods (shoes, a stereo, etc.).

While it may seem like an attractive proposition if you're being picked on, and the inmate offering protection is asking a reasonable price (like a pouch of tobacco a week), there are drawbacks. For example:

- It could be the 'thin end of the wedge' – this week it's a pouch of tobacco, next week it's a pouch *plus* a chocolate bar, and so on.
- Other inmates might consider you 'weak' for choosing this option.
- If the inmate protecting you suddenly leaves or moves unit (he gets caught with drugs, his parole comes through, he gets into a fight with someone, etc.), then you're alone and may get picked on for choosing to be protected in the first place.
- The protector may suddenly ask you to do something that could jeopardise your parole, or, if you are going to trial or haven't been sentenced, might not help your case in court. For example, if they ask you to hold on to some drugs or contraband for them, and you are unlucky enough to get caught.

It's probably best to thank them but decline the offer. Things could get complicated very quickly. And perhaps you could ask yourself, 'If I am being offered protection by another inmate, maybe it's time to start the ball rolling towards placement in the SNU...' (see Chapter 5 for more advice about SNU and whether it might suit you).

I was offered protection from a fellow inmate. I wasn't getting bashed and people weren't stealing my things, and most of the unit was indifferent towards me, but there were some who took great delight in sneaking up to startle me. It was really no more than playground-type behaviour, and despite the dickheads I did have a few people I could call mates. It was one of these mates who offered me protection. A pouch a week. Thanks to my generous parents, I could have afforded it, but I declined. Primarily because I wanted to be able to say, 'I did all my time in mainstream and never needed to pay for help.' I ended up doing that, though the last eight months were in the SNU. So, although it was technically mainstream, the atmosphere in the SNU was much less tense and people were far more civil to each other. Also, there was something that I know would have felt very...undignified...about having to pay for protection against idiots. There's no doubt that the inmate's heart was in the right place, but in a weird way the offer of protection hurt more than the bullying. I guess it doesn't matter now.

Intimate Contact and Body Exposure

Throughout this book, the *lack* of movie-style sexual assaults has been mentioned. What hasn't been mentioned is the high prevalence of consensual, non-sexual man-on-man (or woman-on-woman) contact. It's natural for everyone to seek human contact, and it isn't exclusively family or a girlfriend/boyfriend who can provide contact and comfort. On the outside it goes by largely unnoticed. For example, if you are in a relationship, there is a strong chance you may share a bed or at least share intimate, physical contact on a regular basis. Single people may get human contact through hugs with family and friends, and the occasional one-night stand. While inside, the opportunity to *see and touch* spouses, girlfriends, boyfriends, family and friends is limited strictly to visits and, as mentioned previously, visits aren't as straightforward as having your people drive up to the jail and knock on the door. Nor are inmates and their visitors allowed extensive hands-on contact with each other. For inmates who are settled, and comfortable with their sexuality, physical contact is provided by each other. You may see inmates resting their heads on other inmates' stomachs or thighs. Sometimes, inmates stroke each other's hair. Hugging is common. Whatever your initial reaction to witnessing this behaviour for the first time, *do not* make insinuations that it's strange or gay or is making you uncomfortable. Remember, it's their house, and you've just arrived. What they are doing does not have a sexual component to it: it's done for basic human contact, and, as your time inside increases, you will see how inmate-on-inmate contact can be comforting and relaxing – even with ASD. There isn't a whole lot to say about this topic, except to emphasise a couple of key points: in a male prison you *will* see men being quite 'tender' with each other. *This says nothing about their sexuality.* If you have been in the unit a while, and you have made friends, and suddenly one of them rests his head on your thigh, what do you do? Well, the best idea is to allow it to happen, even if it makes you uncomfortable. Remember, the inmate doesn't want you to feel uncomfortable, and it's actually a compliment, in the sense that *they* obviously feel comfortable enough in your presence to behave in such a manner. If you don't really like it much at all, it would be a good idea to go outside your comfort zone and challenge yourself. So, let them rest their head; it will help desensitise you to the process. If it's making you very uncomfortable, make an excuse to get up, like saying you're going to make a cup of tea, and when you return, sit with your back to the wall, knees against your chest, and re-engage in the conversation. *If* someone says something about your apparent reluctance to engage in physical contact (which is unlikely), you could say, 'It's not personal, I just have proximity issues.'

I was told I was moving from the first-timers unit, to another unit, which at the time was officially called 'the lifestyle modification unit'. Unofficially, it was called the 'drug unit', or 'rehab unit'. I had forgotten I had even applied to go there, and I had made some good mates in the first-timers unit, so was unsure if this was a good thing or a bad thing. But when I got there, I was glad I had made the choice to apply.

First-timers was a 50-cell unit, doubled-up, so at any given time there were 75–90 inmates, a large portion of whom felt they had something to prove. I had done well in there, had avoided any conflict and by the time I left four months after coming in, I was one of six people who had been there longer than anyone else, so my standing in the social hierarchy was good. The rehab unit was a 20-man unit. It was like heaven compared with the hectic nonsense of first-timers. There is a point to this: moving into this new unit was an eye-opening experience. The inmates were older, more experienced, and although I was there only four months, I learnt a lot. It was also the first unit where I saw overt man-on-man displays of affection. There was no kissing, and no actual sexual favours appeared to take place, because as far as I know none of them was gay.

It wouldn't surprise me if relationships do in fact flourish – they would just be kept very secret. It would be very difficult for inmates to have the time and privacy to sexually express their feelings – the same reason why prison rape/sexual assault doesn't happen in the way the silver screen would have you believe. If I were to speculate, most prison relationships would manifest in a manner more emotional than physical.

Penis presentation

Some inmates have a propensity to expose their penis to other inmates. This is not gay or bisexual behaviour, nor is it aggressive per se. It could only be perceived as aggressive if you have an adverse reaction to it the first time, and then the inmates recognise it as one of your 'buttons' to push. So the first time you see this happen, try to show little or no reaction. And it will be a matter of when, not if. If you find this behaviour offputting, don't make a deal of it – just ignore it. As for doing it yourself, feel free to – *except when a CO might see.* If a female CO happens to witness this behaviour, it will go down badly. Try to keep your private parts just that – private.

Putting People on Show

For some readers, the term 'putting someone on show' will be familiar. For others, a brief explanation may be in order. As the name suggests, the concept involves singling someone out in front of a group of people, and doing or saying something which puts that inmate in a position of humiliation or unwanted exposure. For the inmate with ASD, it's much safer to avoid strong opinions, even if you *know* somebody has said something wrong. Is it worth a punch in the face to prove some spurious point? Of course, there are times when fighting may, oddly, be your best option. But, generally, *don't say or do something that is going to draw attention to another inmate*, regardless of the reason. You may find it happening to you, and you'll understand how unpleasant it is. Nobody suddenly wants half the unit looking at them, wondering about them, laughing at them. So remember the golden rule, and avoid making a fellow inmate feel like they're suddenly the centre of attention.

CHAPTER 15

Interacting with COs and Other Staff

Your personal conduct and how you interact with other inmates will be observed by the COs. Although it's not uncommon to see a CO busy in conversation with a colleague, doing paperwork, using a computer or filling in forms, COs actually have a much better understanding of what's going on in their unit than inmates give them credit for. They know who 'runs' the unit, they know who is being bullied, they usually know who the drug users are, and can take an educated guess who the drug runners are – it's just they can't prove it, and as long as there is a basic level of stability in the unit, what does it matter anyway? So, despite having the potential capability to catch the drug users in the act or perhaps stop a 'shipment' coming in, the prevailing attitude appears to be 'Why bother? Some other inmate will just take his place.'

Having said this, *do not think the COs will put up with any overt crap*. They're outnumbered about 25 to 1, so if they think there's going to be a problem, they deal with it by radioing for back-up. COs also wear devices that set off an alarm if they are horizontal for too long, so, even if *both* COs are knocked to the ground, back-up will be coming.

This chapter looks at some of the issues that can arise between inmate and CO, and how to best avoid/deal with the situation.

Communication/interaction with COs

Your behaviour with the COs could potentially have a detrimental effect on your standing among other inmates. Avoiding this is not difficult. *The no. 1 rule*: COs (screws) are 'the enemy' and there is to be no collaboration with the COs, and no interaction with the COs except for the basics (account balances, getting mail handed to you, etc.). If you remember this, you can't really go wrong. However, don't be rude, unless the CO is rude first (which can be the case – this is jail, not a department store). Even then, try not to take the bait – some COs are *looking* for an excuse to get angry.

Other steadfast rules that apply:

- *Never* shake (or lean in to shake) a CO's hand.
- *Never* shake (or lean in to shake) any staff member's hand (like a fitness instructor, nurse, psychologist, etc.). Volunteers from religious groups who come in are fine to interact with normally, *but they are the only ones*.
- Don't converse with the COs except to answer their questions (not *all* questions, obviously – see no evil, hear no evil, speak no evil) or to request something (like an account balance or a form that isn't in the form rack).
- Don't smile and laugh with them.
- Don't do anything they ask just because they are a CO. Sometimes a request could put you in physical danger from other inmates (see the personal anecdote about being asked to bring medicine balls out of the yard to the COs in Chapter 14).

The Balancing Act

Despite these concrete 'rules', the area of staff–inmate interaction is somewhat grey, which makes it especially difficult for the inmate with ASD. It's grey in the sense that, although inmates expect other inmates to treat the COs with disdain, they also know COs have the power to lock the unit down if they feel an exertion of this power is needed. Therefore, one is expected to achieve the correct balance between appearing *not* to respect the COs and at the same time respecting them sufficiently so there are no 'collective' punishments. Sometimes whole units are locked down because some idiot verbally abused a CO or staff member. This collective punishment for an individual's behaviour is a recipe for disaster, at least for the inmate who did the abusing. There is a high probability they will suffer repercussions, unless they're a lifer or a tougher-than-average inmate. As an inmate with ASD (disclosed or otherwise), it's unlikely you will be either of these things. *Don't give the COs any excuse to punish the unit for your indiscretions.* Finding the annoying, ironic balance mentioned above is important, but not difficult.

Breaches

This book contains an explanation of a breach, plus a personal account of one, so this section looks less at the actual process, and more at what you *don't* do if you are breached:

- If you are being breached, *do not mention any other inmate by name*, even if they haven't done anything wrong. Word will get back to the unit that you dropped a name, and that is not good.
- *Think before you speak*: does what I'm about to say in

232

response to this question have the potential to be misinterpreted? Will I be opening a can of worms? Because if the COs think they have stumbled across an inmate who knows what's going on in the unit, but seems quite timid, they will use this against them. For example, 'Right, if you don't tell us who you know is doing drugs in this unit, we'll move you to such-and-such a unit...' or some other unit known throughout the prison as a dangerous place. Act completely ignorant of all illegal activity.

- *This isn't school or work.* You don't need to impress the people who are in charge. Monosyllabic answers and an aloof attitude are what they see all the time. You should keep up this tradition.
- Even if keeping your mouth shut and refusing to tell the truth puts you in the DU, that's a much, much better outcome than some other inmate being subjected to the DU because you squealed on them (or let slip information you shouldn't have).

Basically, take breaches like a man. Don't try to wiggle out of it, and don't give up a fellow inmate.

Urine Tests (UTs)

UTs have been mentioned before in the book, but this segment is specifically related to how the COs and you can 'work together' to minimise stress. If you have ASD, personal space may be an issue of contention. As such, it doesn't take a genius to realise that asking an inmate with ASD to urinate in a cup with two COs standing about a metre behind them may cause problems. If you do have difficulty urinating with people close by, you might want to do one (or more) of the following:

- If the jail knows about your ASD, ask for a consult with a prison psychologist and express your concern. They may be able to get you some leverage, like a longer time to produce a sample or have the COs wait outside the cell.
- There is actually a condition called shy bladder syndrome (paruresis), and if you can get documents from your doctor *prior* to incarceration, this will further help you convince the jail you're not avoiding urinating because you have something to hide, but rather you simply can't urinate in close proximity to others *and* under time pressure.
- If you are asked to provide a sample, you are allowed an hour to produce it. In that time, drink water until you feel like you are going to vomit. When the feeling passes, drink some more. If all goes well, you should be able to produce a sample within the hour.

Naturally, the COs will be the same gender as you, and although chatting to them *might* make you feel like you're starting to relax (because of the distraction), other inmates are liable to say later, 'Did you hear so-and-so, chatting to the screws like they're old buddies?! We'd better keep an eye on him. He's obviously not to be trusted...'

If you need distraction, try to read something with your spare hand. Basically, it comes down to this: don't cooperate too readily with the COs, but don't be needlessly rude lest they decide a 'collective punishment' is in order. It sounds almost contradictory, and at times it is, *but you will get used to it.*

Conversing with the COs

How much an inmate is 'allowed' to interact with COs can depend largely on the jail, or even the unit you are in.

At the remand jail, the attitude towards screws was far more relaxed. You could exchange a few words (that is, you could have a brief but friendly chat), and no one seemed to mind. At least not in the first-timers unit or the drug rehab unit.

At the reception jail, things were different, and you were expected to have minimal interaction with the COs. I witnessed a couple of inmates assaulted (not seriously, fortunately) because they were 'cheeseballing' with the screws.

Then, at placement jail, it seemed calmer. Granted, inmates didn't have long conversations with screws, and there was often animosity displayed in both directions, but there wasn't the near-hysterical atmosphere of 'us versus them' that was so prevalent in reception jail.

Again, at the risk of sounding like a broken record, watch, listen and learn. Your default position should be 'All COs are bad, and I will be nothing more than polite to them. They are not my friend(s), and others feel this way too.' How much you do or do not interact with COs should be based entirely on observing and mimicking – exactly what people with ASD have done forever.

The Fine Line (Again)

Earlier in the book a first-person account was given about a CO asking an inmate to turn down the TV during headcount (see Chapter 8). As that anecdote explains, nobody was cooperative, and it was ultimately the CO's fault. She was essentially asking somebody to put themselves on show, and thus risk their physical safety. Of course, not all examples of this conundrum are so blatant. For example, you may be wandering past the COs' desk and they'll ask if you can get inmate so-and-so to come and see them for whatever reason. Some inmates will comply, some will just ignore them and some will literally tell them to 'fuck off'. The best approach is to find a middle road. There's no need to swear at the COs like that. That's just unpleasant. However, there is some logic to it, in the sense you don't want to be seen doing the COs' job for them. And if you're an inmate with ASD, eager to please, you may find yourself doing 'helpful' things for the COs, all the while ignorant of the growing animosity towards you. If a CO asks you to fetch a fellow inmate, and they ask nicely, and no aggressive or difficult inmates have overheard, then you could go up to the inmate they requested and quietly tell him the COs want him. *Don't just yell out into the yard*: 'Oi! The screws wanna speak to so-and-so!' The last thing you want to look like is a CO's lackey.

When a Fight Breaks Out (the CO Angle)

With a large percentage of inmates fluent in the language of violence, witnessing a fight is a matter of when, not if. For those with ASD, the most pertinent advice on how to respond when a fight occurs (regarding the COs) is *not* to give them any information, whether it be before or after a fight. For example, if you happen to be privy to the fact there is going to be a fight, by now it should be obvious that you don't alert the COs. That should go without saying. What might be a bit less clear for the same inmate with ASD is what to say about the fight if approached by a CO. What you should say will depend on a few factors:

- Did you actually *witness* the fight?
- Did you see it from beginning to end?
- Did you see the events that preceded the fight?
- Did you see who instigated the fight?

As a rule, you tell them nothing. Not literally *nothing*, as in when they ask you a question you refuse to answer it. While you technically have that right, it isn't the best path to take: it just creates unnecessary tension and gives you a bad standing among staff (as an inmate with ASD, you will want to be known as someone who doesn't make waves, whether it be with COs or fellow inmates). So, if you are asked, simply tell them, 'I didn't see anything.' If they say, 'C'mon, we know you saw *something*. You were out here in the yard...', say, 'Chief, honestly, I was cutting laps, minding my own business, and before I knew it those two were fighting, then you guys came out here. That's it. Really.' Perhaps the most important thing you can then say is 'I don't get involved in other people's business. It's how I was raised.' By stating you don't get involved in other people's business, you will earn respect from the COs. Prison snitches might think they curry favour, but, in truth, no one likes a teller. Plus, if this interaction (or one similar) is overheard by other inmates, that is a valuable bonus.

From a practical standpoint, behaving in the appropriate manner regarding the COs is straightforward:

- Don't try to break up fights – the COs get paid to do that.
- When the back-up arrives (which it always will), they will be hot to trot. That is, they will be full of adrenaline, and some COs don't handle that too well and can get a bit needlessly aggressive. Don't rise to it – just do as you are told and do it promptly. Inmates can and do get breached for 'failing to comply with an instruction or order' because they (deliberately) took their sweet time getting against the wall and interlacing their fingers behind their head.
- Don't make any derogatory or inflammatory remarks about the COs, assuming they won't be able to identify

who said it because of the chaos. It could land the whole unit in hot water, and as you should know by now, collective punishments don't end well for the inmate who caused them.

Basically, when it comes to inmates fighting, you want to be the 'ghost' prisoner – that is, the guy nobody sees, the guy nobody pays any attention to. The same theory applies to the COs. When a fight breaks out, try to make yourself the last thing on their minds.

If a CO is Assaulted

Because of my comparatively short time behind bars, I never witnessed a screw being assaulted, which I consider a good thing because when a screw (or any staff member) gets hit, the unit in which it occurred goes into lockdown for at least 24 hours, usually longer. They take that shit pretty seriously. The inmate will face an 'outside charge', and the courts don't look too favourably on people who have assaulted someone who is, essentially, one of their own (a spoke on the wheel of the justice system).

In lieu of some riveting tale about a screw fighting with an inmate, I will tell you instead about a time the unit next to ours more or less rioted. I say more or less because it wasn't exactly a full-blown riot – in the end only five or six inmates wound up in the DU. But I can imagine the atmosphere in there must have been tense. We saw the turtles (riot squad) come running, followed by about eight or nine screws, so we figured something 'big' must have happened. It's not uncommon to see screws kinda half-running, half-jogging to a code that they know is most likely under control, because if things are out of control, they call a specific code. And to that code they will sprint, because it could (theoretically, at least) escalate into a life-or-death situation.

Not that this was the case here. An inmate I know who was in there told me down at medical it had started with a refusal to follow a direction and gone pear-shaped from there. A screw had hot porridge or something thrown at him, he called a code and that was that. The instigators did time in the DU, and I assume at least one was charged. I don't know for sure.

This story adequately illustrates what happens when a CO is assaulted. But, to be clear:

- A code will be called.
- The unit will go into lockdown.
- The perpetrator will be led out of the unit to the DU in a special hold that makes it nearly impossible to do anything other than cooperate.
- They will be charged with assaulting a CO.
- Sometimes, if a unit looks like it might be at risk of rioting, the entire jail is placed into lockdown. This is a safety measure to stop any 'spread' of en masse rebellion.

Keeping Quiet About COs

This book has mentioned (on more than one occasion!) the importance of turning a blind eye to the activities and behaviours of your fellow inmates. The same principle applies to COs. You will inevitably see COs breaking protocol from time to time, like a CO dozing when it's 2.00 pm and things are quiet. Sure, they're technically breaking some rule/policy, but in the greater scheme of things, does it really matter? It's also possible you may witness a CO (or COs) breaking rules in a much less trivial sense, such as assaulting an inmate or threatening to spread rumours that an inmate is guilty of historical child-sex offences or some other rumour that could very well wind up with this inmate being seriously hurt. These are just examples, and you may find you do all your time without witnessing misconduct, trivial or otherwise.

Regardless of what you see or hear, it's not a good idea to alert management to misconduct by a CO. It would achieve very little in the way of change, as much of this behaviour is systemic and has been going on for decades. More importantly, informing on COs could make you a target, and could put you at risk from both the COs *and* other inmates. All it would take is one small comment from a CO to an inmate, suggesting you are an informant, and your life inside could turn upside down overnight. Basically, it's easier and safer to ignore any misbehaviour by COs. After all, they have the keys, the final say and the power.

CHAPTER 16

Avoiding Confrontation

It's best to avoid confrontation altogether. Some inmates would disagree, but for the inmate with ASD, avoiding violence is your safest bet (unless you happen to be a proficient fighter). First, forget what you see in movies – that nonsense about the protagonist fighting (and of course beating) the 'toughest' inmate within an hour of getting to their unit, and instantly gaining status as the alpha male. This is crazy. First, the inmate who just got his butt kicked might be a lifer. This means the likelihood of swift and intense retribution is higher: he has little to lose, and much to gain, by stabbing his attacker when he sees them again.

Or perhaps the guy who got beaten up is the unit's primary supplier of contraband, and they've just inadvertently cut the supply line. Now there are 12 (at least) angry men looking at them for revenge.

The best approach, in real life, is one you will now be very familiar with: watch, listen and learn. Nobody comes flying through the doors wanting to swing punches randomly. If inmates really did that, the unit would be locked down nearly constantly, because of the high number of inmates coming and going.

Due to the idiosyncratic nature of humans, it would be impossible to write a section that addressed every possible scenario. This section looks at more frequent confrontation scenarios and suggests the best course of action. There is *one* piece of advice that applies to everything throughout this chapter: *never tell on anybody, whether it be an inmate or a CO.*

'Engineering' a Safer Environment

The first thing you can do is apply to go to a unit where violence is less prevalent.

Workers units

Inmates who work (outside their units – in the industrial laundry, with the garden crew, in the kitchen and in industries, etc.) are usually housed together, because it makes coordinating shifts easier. These units often have perks; for example, kitchen workers may have access to a wider variety of food; the garden crew get to roam around the jail; and even laundry and industries workers are grateful to have a job, because a job equals a bigger buy-up each week. Because of these perks, most inmates want to stay in the unit, and they know picking fights will have them kicked out of the unit and they'll lose their job.

Drug rehabilitation units

Inmates in the drug rehab units are almost always privy to perks, like smaller units (20 inmates), and the ability to access programs that will either (a) help with sentencing or (b) accelerate the parole process. Again, if people fight, they get kicked out.

The SNU

The SNU is the quietest of all the units. Because the SNU may also house inmates who have had trouble in other units (trouble with other inmates, not trouble with authorities), they rein their behaviour in because they know they can't risk getting booted out.

In-Unit Precautions

There are measures that can be taken to help the inmate with ASD regardless of what unit you are in. For example, take note of:

- where the COs sit
- what they can (likely) see
- where the cameras are
- where 'blind spots' might exist (these areas will be used for drug activity)
- how much time the COs are 'on the floor' (sometimes they watch from a centralised command centre that can see into multiple units)
- response times to fights.

Soak up as much information you can about the layout of the unit and the timing of inmate and CO movement, but be subtle about it. *Don't sit there with a pad and pen making notes.*

Outside Unit Precautions

As mentioned before, fights happen on walkways, at visits, in medical, during education and at the oval/gym. Until you are settled, avoid unnecessary exposure to unfamiliar territory. Try to educate yourself, mostly through listening, as to where the 'blind spots' are along the walkway. Of course, not all prisons will have blind spots, but many do. Don't ask other inmates where they are; just listen and pay attention. If you feel unsafe along the walkway, and you are moving as a group, stick close (but not too close!) to the COs escorting you.

While I was in the SNU, an inmate arrived with a black eye. He had been in a run-of-the-mill unit, and had mentioned something about drugs a bit too loudly, not knowing there was a screw behind him.

The unit got ramped and, fairly or otherwise, he was blamed. He was walking to the oval a few days later when, just as the group rounded a corner, another inmate attacked, punching him and knocking him to the ground. His injuries looked worse than they were, and after getting to know him, it didn't surprise me he was assaulted.

The attacker was able to get away with it because his cronies formed a 'human shield' to prevent the COs from seeing anything, and the cameras were of no use because the assault was timed to occur in the blind spot. And, of course, the victim knew better than to talk. So nobody was punished, but the inmate wound up with us in the SNU, and within a week had dropped his bravado front and was, well, just a regular guy. The point of this story is: if something has happened and you have pissed off some inmates, don't go to the oval with them. It's stupid. Frankly I'm surprised the victim didn't know better.

Ways to 'Hide'

You can minimise your interaction with inmates by staying in your cell as much as possible. And when you are out, you can stick to yourself and read or work out alone. Other inmates do this, and not necessarily because they want to avoid interaction

– some may be on sedating medication, others may be feeling unwell, others may just enjoy solitude. Provided you're polite when you are out of your cell and follow prison 'rules' (like turning a blind eye to drug use and suchlike), nobody is going to really notice (or care) if you spend a lot of time alone. Regardless of how much time you spend in your cell, knowing the basics of avoiding conflict is important.

Verbal Communication

Somebody once said language is the first weapon drawn in a conflict, and this adage remains true inside. Language extends to non-verbal forms of communication, like body language and the written word. Fights can break out because an inmate looked at someone 'the wrong way' or found out via correspondence that another inmate had been talking negatively about them. While you are still adapting to prison life (or even adapting to a new unit), remember: what's been said *cannot* be unsaid. To play it safe, say very little. But, as mentioned in earlier chapters, don't be *so* reluctant to talk that people think you have something to hide. It may seem like a tightrope, and at time it feels like one, but you will learn to balance. Everyone does.

If someone is in jail, as opposed to a psychiatric facility, it would be safe to assume they have at least a very basic understanding of social rules and etiquette. If they don't, they usually learn quickly, either through threats or actual violence. But some people…they, well, they just don't seem to get it, no matter how much crap they cop. This was the case with an inmate who arrived in the SNU with an overtly puffed-up face

– he'd recently had an operation to re-align his jaw, after it was broken by another inmate in a run-of-the-mill unit.

I initially felt for the guy. He seemed okay at first, although a little bit stupid. Which is not necessarily a problem – there are plenty of inmates with average or below-average intelligence who get along just fine. The problem with this guy was he just didn't seem to learn from his experience. Ever.

Even in the SNU, he was assaulted five times (none of them serious attacks – SNU fights are comparatively tame). I watched with interest as it played out: he would say something obnoxious and unprovoked, and he would be ignored. He would do it again, and be told to shut up. Then he would do it again, and be warned there could be physical repercussions. And then he would do it again! It was a bizarre phenomenon to observe. And he wasn't a sadomasochist who wanted to be hurt – every time he was assaulted he'd run to the screws and promptly tell on the person who had (understandably) thumped him.

He single-handedly got five inmates kicked out of the SNU, all because of his atrocious communication skills. We were all glad to see the back of him when he was released.

Most inmates with ASD will adapt to their surroundings, especially if they (again!) watch, listen and learn. Some inmates, however, seem intent on wearing a metaphorical blindfold and earmuffs, and always believing they are in the right, irrespective of how many times they're proved wrong.

Guidelines for Neutral Communication

Listen – *really* listen. When engaging with another inmate, try to turn down the volume of the internal commentary we all have running through our heads. Focus on what they're saying, rather than what your response will be.

- Don't interrupt – in jail people tell stories of their 'glory days' as a criminal and can get quite animated. Suddenly saying 'I wonder what's for lunch today?' when they're in the thick of their story is poor form.
- Don't mumble under your breath – even if it's not about an inmate (you may be griping about the food, etc.), others might not see it that way.
- Don't give unsolicited advice – if someone is asking for advice, that will be clear.
- Don't interject – you may be reading a book or just sitting against the yard wall, relaxing, and you overhear a conversation that interests you – *don't go and invite yourself in*. Not only might some inmate be cross you invited yourself into their discussion, but it may seem like you actually *are* listening to conversations when you sit outside with a book. People with ASD know they can do both – read and pay attention to what's around them – but while in jail, act like all you are focusing on is your book (or the TV, or cutting laps or staring out into the distance, deep in your own thoughts).
- Forget principles – prison conversations are usually quick, rapidly change direction and don't dwell on any one topic for very long. If something is said that you feel strongly about, just leave it be, at least for the moment. People with ASD are often principled people, binary people. Not being able to say your piece is frustrating, but just deal with it. No one is expecting you to abandon your beliefs, just don't rub them in other inmates' faces.
- The last word – some people with ASD have a propensity to want 'the last word' and/or to 'get closure' on a topic. Forget all that. Don't dominate conversations, and at the end of the day ask yourself: do you really think it's worth potentially fighting someone, serving time in the DU and

losing other privileges, just to prove some essentially innocuous point?

- Agree to disagree – there is absolutely no need to bother trying to correct another inmate's tightly held beliefs. Trivial things are fine to joke about, but topics like families, other inmates, politics and religion are better left alone.

When I was in the drug rehab unit at the remand jail, I would take advantage of the old (but functioning) exercise bike in the yard. One day I was halfway through my 20-minute ride when I heard a group of inmates, who were sitting close by, talking about a topic familiar to me. I interjected. Well, I actually answered a question for them. Everything seemed fine. Or so I thought.

A couple of days later I made a benign comment to one of these guys and he got cross and said, 'Who are you to make these comments? We weren't talking to you. Mind your own business.' He was a bit more colourful in his language, but you get the drift. Instead of being angry, or hurt, I took his advice/ insight on board and made a vow never again to interject in a conversation. He was right, after all. It wasn't my business. And they weren't talking to me. So I was able to assimilate his advice and I think it served me well. Now, I'm passing it on to others.

- Avoid being facetious or sarcastic – complex or subtle forms of sarcasm or facetiousness can be completely misunderstood. Inmates with ASD may need to make a conscious effort to 'tone down' intellectualism. Here's an example of facetiousness being misunderstood.

One day during my time in placement jail, there was a contractor standing outside my cell, fixing the plumbing or something. Being bored prisoners, we watched him through the window. It wasn't very entertaining. After a couple of minutes, Stringers decided to take his penis out, to try to distract the worker or for whatever reason it is grown men get their penises out in inappropriate settings. Anyway, the worker took no notice and we decided to go into the yard for a smoke. On the way, another inmate, Rory, nudged me and whispered, 'Whaddya reckon? Stringers' cock isn't bad, eh?' Now, I am quite certain Rory isn't gay, nor is Stringers. But my response, said in a very facetious manner, was: 'Yeah…it was just…wow. I'm set for tonight, that's for sure.' I knew Rory understood I was joking, and Stringers wasn't paying attention, but this other dingbat with us, GG, thought I was actually making a serious remark and said, 'Oh my God! Did you hear that?! Holy shit! Will likes cock! Will's a fag!'

I didn't bother refuting the point. I'm a comfortable heterosexual who doesn't give two hoots about somebody's sexuality (or what GG thought about mine). But this story illustrates how a simple, innocuous comment can fly straight over the heads of some inmates. So, until settled, operate under the assumption that the median level of intelligence isn't all that high. I understand that sounds almost judgemental, but this book is based on my experiences inside, neither embellished nor trivialised.

Nervousness

For people with ASD reading this, you will be familiar with the increased heart rate, butterflies in the stomach and dread you sometimes feel when you know it's time to socialise, and you have little choice but to join in. What will be new for you is interacting with inmates. Frustratingly, when you arrive as a new inmate, the predatory inmates will, at some point, strike up a conversation with you to try to ascertain whether you're:

- a threat
- neutral (meaning you will fight if challenged but otherwise mind your own business)
- 'weak' (meaning you are unlikely to want to fight and will try avoiding this at all costs).

How you talk to these inmates can form an opinion that may be difficult to change retrospectively. That is, if you appear scared and 'weak' when you first arrive, it's unlikely the unit populace will believe you if you start acting 'tough' a week later. The best way to deal with this is to be polite but keep to yourself. Be taciturn with your responses when being questioned by another inmate. These will be questions about:

- what you're in for
- where you're from
- who you know inside jail
- who you know outside jail – other criminals, etc.
- which units you've been in
- whether you've done time before
- how long you have to go.

It's deeply ironic – inmates say they loathe the police, yet the first thing these same individuals do as soon as someone new walks through the unit door is interrogate them. You may feel like pointing that out to them, but it's best kept to yourself. When subjected to this questioning, just answer honestly. If you don't know anyone they know, so what? The world's a big place. Just play their little game – it won't last long.

Trying to Keep Cool if Confronted

Nervous people can lose their skills of articulation. Being confronted by an inmate is a nerve-wracking experience, but only to a point. It's only as nerve-wracking as you *allow* it to be. That will be cold comfort for people with ASD reading this, but that's only because prison is just a construct in your mind at this point. Once actually there, you may surprise yourself with your ability to assimilate, especially if you implement what you have read in this book. Try to remember these key points. Some people with ASD experience a sense of calm when under pressure. If this is you, that's a significant advantage for jail. For those who don't experience this calm:

- Focus on breathing. Keep your heart rate slow.
- Remember, this inmate is a human, not a super-strong cyborg under living human tissue à la *The Terminator.*
- There are *two* of you. Therefore, you control 50 per cent of what happens. This is particularly important to remember, because at times you will feel like they are 100 per cent in control. *They are not.*
- If they are making unreasonable demands, draw strength from it. *Turn fear into anger.*
- Keep your voice low. This suggests confidence and shows a degree of respect.
- Most face-to-face confrontations *don't* end in violence, especially if you make it clear you're not going to be drawn into some bullshit non-issue.

Hot-Button Topics and Areas of Expertise

Certain topics elicit strong emotional responses. It's important you don't forget where you are and allow your passion to transcend social protocol, such as having an argument over your hot-button issue(s). It could turn physical, and you (or they, or both of you) could get seriously injured over differing opinions. This applies to topics of expertise as well. As mentioned in an earlier chapter, people with ASD have areas of knowledge that go far beyond a fleeting interest. Do your best to keep talk about your SI to a minimum. As mentioned earlier, coming across as preoccupied with a certain topic is akin to preaching, and this won't help you make friends. Only talk about a topic as much as anyone else does.

Different Jails, Different Fightin' Words

Occasionally you will see an inmate say something to another inmate, and suddenly they're at each other's throats, only for it to be stopped by a third inmate, which is technically against jailhouse 'rules', as protocol dictates inmates don't get involved in other people's fights. The reason the third inmate got involved is because something has likely been said that is acceptable in a particular state or territory's jail system, but not where you are (or the other way around). For example:

I was introduced to an inmate who went by the name 'Letters'. He was called this, presumably, because he had a series of seemingly random letters tattooed across his body, including his face.

Letters had done time in a jail down south. These jails were generally considered more dangerous – although this would always depend on who you talk to.

One day, out in the yard, one of his friends joked about him being 'suss' (meaning 'suspect' or 'suspicious'). In this jail, calling someone suss, when you are clearly joking, is acceptable. It could start a fight if you called someone you didn't know 'suss', but otherwise it wasn't a fightin' word. Well, Letters was conditioned to interpret it as fightin' words.

Luckily, it was all explained by the inmate who intervened, and they didn't come to blows. The moral of the tale is never make assumptions about how inflammatory words will be received, so err on the side of caution and don't use them.

Non-Verbal Communication

A lot of communication between humans is non-verbal. For example, eye contact plays a huge role in how we perceive people's reactions and emotions. In jail, prolonged eye contact is a clear sign of confrontation, so don't engage in it. And, as mentioned earlier in the book, if someone thinks you are staring at them, just say, 'Did you go to such-and-such a school?' or, if the age gap is bigger, ask, 'Did you used to live on such-and-such a street?' There are many variations you can use, but only one main goal: make them believe you mistook them for somebody you know and apologise if they thought you were staring. If someone is staring at you, here are some tips:

- First, try to establish they are in fact looking at you. It might be that you are sitting under the communal TV or a clock. If they *are* almost certainly looking at you:
    - Ignore it. Ignore it completely. Don't look back at them – that's what they want you to do.
    - Move out of their line of vision. Do this subtly, like make a tea and then move to your table to drink it, or go outside if the staring is occurring inside.
- If the staring persists, it will feel very awkward, but you may need to address it head on. Walk up to them and ask something benign like 'Do I know you?' or 'Is there something you wanna ask or tell me? Because I couldn't

help but notice you keep looking at me...' For better or worse, this will bring the issue out into the open, which is a step closer to resolving it.

The idea of having to confront another inmate may seem very scary, but it may also be the single best thing you can do.

Physical Communication

There are specific things inmates do to communicate physically. The most common (and overt) form this takes is an inmate invading your personal space, even if they're asking to borrow a pen or something equally as innocuous. This is no accident. They are deliberately doing it to 'remind' you of your social standing. Try your best to avoid stepping backwards. It's difficult but not impossible.

Another form of dominant behaviour is an inmate placing a leg up on a chair when you're sitting at a table. This allows them to look down at you (in a literal sense), and essentially place their genitals close to your head, which is a provocative act of domination – a classic 'alpha male' gesture. *Ignore this if it happens to you, and, more importantly, don't do it to other inmates. They may interpret this as a clear sign of confrontation and may want to take it further.*

Conciliatory Gestures/Language

If you have ASD, using submissive communication, both verbal and physical, is a familiar feeling. Jails are often reminiscent of primary school, especially the primitive social pecking order based on who could beat whom in a fight. Fighting is something that *doesn't* have to happen – there are inmates who do sentences of three to five years without getting into a fight. This is usually because they're naturally tough and confident. But lacking these qualities does not automatically mean you will become a communal punching bag.

Find your rung on the social ladder – as mentioned before, you don't even have to *win* a fight to gain respect – you gain that by keeping your mouth shut when questioned by the COs. The anecdote at the end of Chapter 5 is a real-life illustration of this concept. If you are challenged, use the gestures that come naturally: open arm stance, distancing yourself from the agitator and steady (but not confrontational) eye contact.

While in the middle of a workout, in a new unit (I had been there less than a week), I was confronted by this idiot in the yard. He saunters up, asking, 'What have you been saying behind my back? What? You can't say it to my face?'

I had literally no idea at all what he was talking about, but I was using conciliatory gestures (arms open, palms up), which I hadn't even noticed until he hissed, 'Put your arms down. The screws will see.' Then, as quickly and surprisingly as he had confronted me, he changed his tune. 'Nah, I was just muckin' with ya. It's all sweet.' He then turned around and left, leaving me feeling weak at the knees, shaking and nauseous.

I later realised what he was doing, because I saw him do it to other new arrivals. He would do the whole 'So-and-so said you said this blah blah…' to see if the new arrival would want to fight simply because they had been challenged. I never saw anyone take him on.

He was a bored, aggressive, hyperactive killer with over a decade to go before he was even eligible for parole – I suppose violence was normal for him. It coursed through his veins, much like the gutter drugs he regularly pumped into them.

You don't have to act tough – sometimes acting submissive

is best. Jail is about survival, and if being self-deprecating, not pretending to be tough and being a good-natured guy works for you, run with it. It worked for me.

Don't Lose Hope

Life behind bars can be violent and scary, but it's better you hear the truth than some fairytale. If you're an adept fighter, you may find jail easier than you expected. If you *can* fight, keep it on the down-low. You don't want to invite challengers. Most inmates can pick good fighters by the way they carry themselves, but generally don't challenge them just for the sake of it – you'd need to give them a reason, and this book will help you understand how to avoid this. But never forget: everyone is doing it hard in jail. Having and holding on to a sense of compassion for your fellow inmates is important for your humanity and sense of self. If you *can* fight, refrain from going on about it.

If you aren't a fighter, don't lose hope: there are plenty of inmates who are just like you. The important thing is to gauge a situation for the best possible outcome, which is almost always *not* fighting. The chances of you leaving jail in a bodybag are very, very slim. Try to keep this knowledge front and centre – the odds are on your side.

The Gamble

It would be irresponsible to tell readers who may be facing time to enter jail with a 'I'll get them before they get me' attitude. And besides, as mentioned earlier, trying to take out the 'biggest dude in the unit' is Hollywood nonsense. However, the following *isn't* Hollywood nonsense:

1. If challenged, swinging first and asking questions later can be the best approach. When inmates see you are willing to fight (even if you aren't particularly adept at it), you may have literally *one* fight in the entire duration of your sentence. The bullies will move on to someone else.
2. Be assertive from day dot. Don't let anyone stand over you. Be polite and respectful, but draw the line at taking any bullshit. Easier said than done, but possible. Very possible. As mentioned above, one crowded, hectic minute could put you in good stead for months or years of incarceration.

This section is comparatively short. An entire *chapter* could be devoted to the 'pre-emptive strike' and 'being assertive from day dot' methods. The reason there isn't such a chapter is because people with ASD aren't naturally inclined to fight. And if we were, there would be no need for this book at all. Violence should be a last resort, even though the 'pre-emptive strike' theory contradicts this. It may sound confusing, but you will pick up the social nuances of confrontation quickly, even if it's only through observation. If you know how to fight, you don't really need too much help in this area. For the rest, the key is knowing your place and trusting your instincts.

Only in retrospect was I able to truly see where I should have thumped another inmate, or said this, or ignored that. But hindsight is always 20–20. And when it came to 'seeing' social situations unfurling between me and another inmate (or inmates), I was nervous, unsure and far from confident.

Over time I began to understand how to pick up the subtleties, but that didn't mean I made no social mistakes. The difference was that by then I knew how to deal with it in a non-violent matter (except when I got bopped in the face because I stood up to a bully).

Watch, listen, learn – I wish I had been told this before I went inside. That's why I have mentioned it ad nauseum.

And try to never, ever let somebody dictate your emotions. If bullying is becoming a problem, ask to move units, or, better yet, try for the SNU. You could do your whole time in mainstream (provided your offence doesn't involve children), and do it the easy way, instead of enduring the needlessly difficult Bronx units.

All my time was spent in mainstream, about a third of it in the SNU. Comparatively speaking, the SNU was wonderful.

Finally

Most new inmates are nervous when coming into jail. Having ASD will exacerbate this, but it doesn't have to *define* it. The best way to avoid conflict in a violent place like jail is to:

- get yourself into the SNU or equivalent as soon as possible
- don't just dive in – *stand back, watch a little, learn a little*
- avoid drugs
- keep strong opinions to yourself
- say too little rather than too much
- always keep prison politics within the confines of the inmate population – not for COs' ears
- don't pretend to be tough.

Naturally there's only so much a book can do to help you inside, but if you try to keep what you have learnt at the forefront of your decision-making, it will give you a significant head start.

CHAPTER 17

Coping Mechanisms

All people with ASD use coping mechanisms, even if they haven't had an official diagnosis of ASD. Coping mechanisms can be very individualistic. If you have particular mechanisms that might appear 'odd' to other inmates (such as humming, thumbsucking or overt rocking back-and-forth), save these for your cell. Otherwise, feel free to engage in soothing behaviour, provided it doesn't interfere with other inmates. For example, no one is going to give you a hard time if you practise meditation or tai-chi. In fact, if they see you are genuine about it, and do it regularly, inmates will respect it.

Provided here is an outline of different coping mechanisms. This is a guide only. As time goes on, you will naturally start to engage in behaviours that help you cope with the stresses of jail.

Practical Action

A room for one
It would be a lie to say you are guaranteed to be in a cell by yourself. But there's a decent chance you will land in one anyway

(not *all* jails suffer from overcrowding), and if you *are* doubled-up, use your diagnosis to try to manipulate the system into providing you with a (much-needed) single cell.

Put in a request to see the mental health team, and tell them the truth: you have ASD, and sharing a cell means no meaningful time to yourself. Too much time spent like this will likely result in avoidable stress for you.

You may *feel* like you've come up against a brick wall but keep on chipping away at it. There are inmates who are not allowed to be doubled-up – you can become one of them. But remember to be polite. Firm, but polite. Show them you're serious about the need to be singled out by gently but relentlessly reminding the mental health team.

Your Special Interest (SI)

One of the defining characteristics of ASD is having a 'special interest' – an interest in a topic (or topics) that goes deeper than most neurotypical people experience. For example, a neurotypical football fan might be able to tell you who's captain of their favourite team, where they are on the ladder, when they last won the Premiership and name most of the players on the team. The fan with ASD could tell you what each player had for breakfast on the morning of their last Premiership, where each player was born, when the club was founded, how long the founder's beard was and the temperature in Venezuela on the day the club played its first game. This might be a *tiny* bit exaggerated, but not by much. Our SIs allow us to escape into a safe place – the psychological opposite of how jail might make you feel.

While access to material about your SI may be curtailed inside jail, it doesn't have to be eliminated. It's a matter of lowering your expectations: instead of eagerly awaiting the next episode of your favourite show, get your people to send you a poster of the show's cast, and some information from the internet about the show. You can also talk to one of your people who shares similar interests to you – even if it's not your favourite SI. Learn to make do with less – that, really, is the very crux of jail.

Find sanctuaries

Everybody needs sanctuaries, especially people with ASD. Finding sanctuaries in a place like jail may seem far-fetched, but it's not as difficult as you think. Logically, the best sanctuary is your cell. But because you're not able to pick and choose your cell time, it's important to engineer other sanctuaries. Find a place where you can read that is quiet. There may be other inmates utilising the same space for the same reason, but it's jail – compromises must be made. *The book you're reading is your sanctuary.*

Mindfulness, a concept discussed later, is central to making the most of your sanctuaries. If you can master the art of creating a sanctuary *within* yourself, your lack of creature comforts will seem trivial. Sitting in a corner in the yard, with the sun on your face, a book in your hand and peace in your mind: that is, in fact, a sanctuary (albeit temporary).

Drawing, writing and music

Art helps us express ourselves, explore emotions and try to make sense of the world. In prison, you may feel your world has been inverted, and this can be very disconcerting, especially for the inmate with ASD. Expressing yourself creatively can help you assimilate and relax. You can do this almost straight away, with the paper and pens you were issued upon arrival. Drawing or writing how you feel will bring you closer to resolving negative issues.

Some jails run music classes and allow inmates to take acoustic guitars back to their units. If this sounds good to you, use the 'general request' form to ask about music programs. Listening to music you like is another effective coping strategy, so if you have the means (and the jail permits it), order a discman (or CD player) and some CDs you like. Music can take you to places far beyond the confines of jail.

Use writing to keep track of your moods – patterns may emerge. But remember, any 'personal' writing (that is, anything other than forms, legal documents or parole correspondence) should be done in your cell. You don't want inmates thinking you're writing about them.

Continue intellectual development

Not only is keeping your mind active good for boredom, it's also an effective coping mechanism. If you have your mind preoccupied with a course, even if it's an easy course you may never use (like traffic controlling), you will still benefit from the mental distraction it provides. There's also the possibility of tertiary courses if you are going to be inside for long enough.

Helping other inmates with legal work and parole applications can also keep you intellectually stimulated. A busy mind is a happy mind. Try your best to have *some* form of intellectual stimulation daily, even if it's 'just' a game of Scrabble.

Talk to the professionals

If your mood is low almost all the time, don't be afraid to reach out for help. As discussed in Chapter 7, there will be a mental health team whose sole purpose is to help inmates like you. Talking to them can be very beneficial, and can help in the following areas:

- Fast-tracking you to a single-bed cell (if you aren't in one already).
- Getting you magazine articles, books or CDs about your SI.

- Making sure you see the psychiatrist sooner rather than later.
- If your low mood is attributable to living in a run-of-the-mill unit, they may discuss the option of moving you to the SNU or equivalent.

If the mental health team know about your diagnosis, and see you taking pro-active steps to minimise negative experiences, they are likely to make a genuine effort to help you.

Physical Approach

Tony didn't have ASD, at least not to my knowledge, but he was a good mate, and we shared a mutual hatred of violence and bullying. Tony's adherence to his goal of losing weight was nothing short of awe-inspiring. He had spent his whole life overweight, right up until he was sent to jail for drug trafficking. It was at this point he saw a great opportunity to make use of all the free time and get fit. He made it his goal to lose weight, and he was serious about it. In the five months we lived together he lost about 15 kg. More impressive still, and more to the point, he had chosen to create a goal for himself, and come hell or high water, he was gonna get there.

I include this anecdote to illustrate how making a decision to improve yourself – whether physically, mentally, emotionally or socially – can make your time go faster, make you more productive and give you a real sense of achievement. Having an ongoing goal in jail can be helpful for your mood. I chose to try to build as much muscle as possible while inside, and it kept me busy, and when I could actually see the improvements, it inspired me further.

Diet and Exercise

You will see some very fit people in jail, and you will also see some very *unfit* people too. Having a healthy diet and exercise regime is good for many reasons, but its most important function is improving your outlook on life. Aside from giving you something positive to focus on, diet and exercise will:

- release endorphins
- provide energy, not take it
- give you a healthy hobby.

Moreover, exercise is a quick, efficient way to lift one's mood, and lift it significantly.

Sometimes I would call Mum in the mornings, feeling pretty low but not having anyone else I felt I could talk to. She would almost always ask if I had done a workout yet. Usually, when I was whingeing and carrying on, I hadn't. She'd tell me to call back after some exercise.

It didn't take us long to notice the direct correlation between exercise and my outlook on the day. I cannot stress strongly enough the benefits of having an exercise regime while locked up.

Exercise as a Natural Antidepressant

If you put in the effort, you'll see the benefits. And this will make you want to exercise more. It's a positive cycle. It also provides a sense of control: what you eat, how much cardio you get and how much muscle-building you do. Inmates often work out solo, so your ASD will have little impact. You won't stand out because you train alone. Just remember to follow the guidelines about working out – see Chapter 12.

Yoga

Some more progressive prisons offer yoga as an activity. If not, you can order mats to exercise on, and the yard often has larger gym mats for inmates to sit on. Theoretically, if you have the funds, you could order a CD-playing device, some yoga instruction CDs, and teach yourself yoga. That's why building a rapport with the mental health team is a good idea, because they can offer help with this type of thing. They may already have some instructional CDs or literature. Doing yoga in the yard is unlikely to bring unwanted attention. You're not hurting anyone and, if you're tucked away in a corner, you aren't in anyone's way.

Sleeping Easy

Sleep hygiene can play a big role in your mental health and, by proxy, your ability to cope. People with ASD can suffer from sleep problems, such as:

- a delay in falling asleep
- frequent waking
- inadequate duration of sleep.

Jail can exacerbate these traits, so doing what you can to get a good night's sleep is important.

- Try not to lie in bed watching TV. Sit on the stool for that (or sit on the mattress – just don't snuggle under the covers and watch the screen).
- Don't snack in bed.
- Keep your sheets clean (weekly cleaning is enough).

If you are tossing and turning, turn on your light and read. Don't just toss and turn relentlessly. It makes the minutes seem like hours, and in the watches of the night small problems can morph into big ones, and before you know it you have thought yourself into whirlwind of worry. Distract yourself – it's better than dwelling on negative things.

The Sun

If you are lucky enough to land in a jail that offers plenty of yard time, *and* the yard gets sunlight, use it. Sunlight is thought to trigger the release of a neurotransmitter called serotonin. Many of the more widely prescribed antidepressants like fluoxetine (Prozac) and paroxetine (Paxil) work by elevating levels of this chemical. Irrespective of whether you are on these medications or not, you will still benefit from time in the actual sun. Just don't overdo it. Between 15 and 20 minutes per day is ideal.

Social Interaction

Feelings of animosity towards people in jail are common. Whether it's a staff member or an inmate, adopting a philosophical approach to social interaction is a very important tool. *If you can learn to let the crap just wash over you, feelings of animosity won't be able to stick, and that will make your time inside easier.*

What's discussed in the following section is for the benefit of your mental health, rather than avoiding trouble or appeasing people.

> **Please note**
> The examples given here are of exchanges between you and COs. But the principles remain applicable to exchanges with inmates too.

When a CO Insults You

At some point during your incarceration, you can expect to receive some abuse from the COs. If a CO insults you, the best approach is to completely ignore it, as if it had never been said at all. If the insult is in the form of a question, say something non-committal. COs can get fruity with their language and very aggressive with their insinuations and/or outright statements (see the anecdote about the CO making insinuations regarding rape in Chapter 14). And remember, sometimes they *want* a rise out of you. *Don't give them the satisfaction.*

Power-Hungry COs

Some COs seem intent on antagonising inmates. If they worked in an airport, they'd probably belittle the passengers. If they worked as police, they would probably give you a swift punch to the ribs if you challenged them. It's just their nature. The problem for people with ASD is that it's *our* nature to bottle up emotions. But, as you have almost certainly experienced before, bottling up emotions is not the most effective way to deal with stress. We're liable to pop, like a balloon, if pushed too far. *You do not want to 'pop' in jail. It will end badly.*

I knew that Max had ASD. He had told me. He'd been diagnosed when he was about 13 or 14. We talked about having ASD, and how jail wasn't always easy because of it. He was a nice guy. At the time I was doubled-up with the unofficial 'head' of the unit, and he told me Max was being 'reintegrated' into the prison population after having spent nearly four months in solitary for assaulting a screw.

Talking to Max, you wouldn't think he would be the sort to assault a screw. He obviously had 'popped', and it was a screw who had been holding the pin. One day, when the jail was going into lockdown for staff training, the COs asked us to muster up. They spent longer than usual doing the count. Sometimes that just happens. But this seemed to really distress and anger Max, because he suddenly blurted out, 'What's the fucking problem? How fucking hard can it be to count!? What the hell is wrong with you guys?!' They told him to shut up, which he did, but he still looked angry.

We all got locked away, and I decided to stay awake rather than sleep, for no reason other than I wanted to work out when we were released and didn't want to have to shake off that 'post-sleep' grogginess before exercise. About an hour after lockaway, the screws who had been on during muster, accompanied by two more screws, came into the unit. They headed straight for Max's cell. You didn't have to be a qualified psychiatrist to know it was going to end badly.

I heard the whole thing. The screw had a valid point, and I understand why he wanted to say what he did. But he pushed Max just that bit too far. I could hear it in Max's voice. He was inflating, and quickly. He was about to pop. Then he did.

Next thing there's a code being called, Max is screaming, there are punches being thrown left and right. It was a mess. The turtles came flying in, batons at the ready. Those turtles were nuts. Frankly I'm glad I was locked safely in my cell.

Anyway, they subdued him, dragged him off and that was the last time I saw Max. It wasn't the last time I heard him, though. When I would go to medical in the afternoons, sometimes the turtles would walk through the waiting room towards the cells at medical. When the door was open, we could hear him cussing and carrying on. He was like a wild animal, and they treated him like one.

I'm no mental health professional, but there had to be a better way to treat Max than what was going on. It was a vicious and completely unnecessary approach to dealing with the situation.

The point is: try and allow the COs' negativity to just 'flow over' you. Don't let them get the better of you. Just focus on keeping your own thoughts clean and clear.

C and C

There's a theory about dealing with social situations that make you frustrated or angry. Put simply, it's the *'Curiosity and Compassion'* approach, and it means just what it sounds like: approach other people with interest and kindness. It will take some practice, but it's worth it in the long run. It's not the same as pity – it's not condescending or meant to belittle the person. Rather, it's about being humanitarian. *If you can see them for the human they are, you're essentially disarming them of their power.* Because they're not robots, they have hopes, dreams, fears, inadequacies. If you can view them like this, even the most antagonistic CO will elicit feelings of curiosity (and possibly sympathy), rather than anger.

Old Friends

Maintain contact with positive people you knew *before* prison. Hearing their voice and listening to them talk about normal things in the outside world will help you. You might think hearing people talk about the outside would be hard to hear, but it's the opposite. It keeps you grounded, reminds you of what lies ahead and, most important of all, it reminds you people care.

Minimising Negative Thinking

Going from freedom to incarceration is a lot to deal with, and you will likely experience negative thoughts related to the sudden and intense change in environment. All inmates experience this. But while neurotypical inmates are assimilating into their environment, ASD inmates are slowly being identified as 'different'. This is when things can start to become tricky. But don't despair – you have time on your side too. Watch, listen, learn. Employ the techniques described in this book.

Learn to feel free in your mind. If that proves to be difficult, because the harassment is relentless, *use your diagnosis to pry open the door to a quieter environment*. If you must wait, or if it seems there really *isn't* an SNU or equivalent (very, very unlikely), here are some examples of how you can minimise negative thinking

TV shows

It's strange, almost surreal, listening to a cold-blooded killer talk about their excitement regarding the upcoming events on a soap opera. But jail is a strange place, and expect some inmates, especially those doing longer sentences, to be into soap opera-type TV shows. Obviously, not all inmates watch fictional, traditionally structured narratives, but a lot do. It can give you something to look forward to, something simple and straightforward. A way to just turn off your brain for a while and let it soak in the soothing glow of Tinsel Town. TV is a form of CBT, and if you are lucky enough to have a TV in your cell, make the most of it. If you *don't* have a TV, the next best thing for this is a good book.

Please note
If your crime has generated a degree of interest from the media, and you have had your image shown on TV, you may consider avoiding television *altogether*, at least initially. Watching TV may bring back unwanted memories of media harassment.

Music

Music is more than just a way to distract yourself. Studies have shown that music can release feel-good chemicals, much like the post-workout 'high' people feel after exercise. Evolution has taught us to recognise patterns – night and day, the seasons, when trees produce fruit, when animals eat, where they eat and so on. Brain scans conducted on volunteers while they listened to music showed the area of the brain responsible for recognising patterns would light up. Then, the brain gives itself a 'mental high-five' by releasing feel-good chemicals (dopamine, serotonin, endorphins) so you continue to look for and assimilate patterns.

If you can purchase a stereo and CDs on STP (see Chapter 11), music can be an effective means to escape from negative thoughts.

Warm and fuzzy thoughts

Every night, while I was falling asleep, I would think about my niece, who was only a baby. By the time I finished jail, she was talking. I would ring my sister (my relationship with

271

whom had flourished since she knew I was truly drug-free)
just to hear my little niece in the background. Then I started
to think about her simple world – free, full of new and exciting
things. It didn't make me bitter or feel sorry for myself; quite
the opposite. It was the same talking to my parents. I always
thought hearing about people's lives on the outside would be
like rubbing salt into the wound, but it isn't.

If you can get photos of family, friends or pets sent in, do so. Sometimes getting photos of children into jail can be tricky, because society protects its most vulnerable members. Usually, a signed affidavit is required from the child's parents or caregivers before photos of children make it into your cell. Keep all letters, cards and photos from family and friends. Look at them from time to time. This will give you strength.

Count your blessings

Be grateful for all you can be. Jail is not a fun place, but it doesn't have to be the armpit of the universe either. Try starting a 'Grateful' list and add one thing a day to it. Just one thing you are grateful for. It could be something that happened that day, or something you realise you're *ongoingly* grateful for. Watch the list grow. This is a tangible, personal and easily accessible reminder that you still have positive thoughts and things to be grateful for.

An effective way of identifying what you should be grateful for is differentiating between a right and a privilege. Without going into needless detail listing all the different rights/privileges you will experience in jail, just keep in the back of your mind that there are some things you *need*, while others you really just *want*. And if something *is* a privilege, treat it as such. The unhappier inmates are often those who feel the world owes them.

Mental Strategies to Help Detach and Stay Positive

There is a difference between minimising negative thinking and detaching from it. Detaching is just one step further. It would be great to remain detached for the duration of your sentence, but that's not possible. In lieu of that, here are some tips to help you put up a psychological barrier against negative thoughts and feelings.

Lose yourself

Books, magazines and TV are the most commonly used tools to detach from your inner dialogue. In jail, it's also the easiest way. Except, of course, for drugs, which, as discussed before, are a stupid (and dangerous) way to spend your time. TV and books are *designed* to take you away to another place. But they're not the only way you can achieve this.

Solution-based therapy

If there's an issue that's taking up a lot of (negative) thinking time, and it's based around indecision, solution-based therapy (SBT) is an effective, quick exercise you can do in your cell. For example, imagine you're deciding whether or not to hold another inmate's contraband while he goes to visits. He usually carries it on him but can't risk taking it there. It's Monday night, and his visit is on Tuesday. You've said you'll give him an answer in the morning. That night, grab some paper and:

- brainstorm ideas (what could go wrong, what are the benefits – anything you feel is relevant)
- whittle down your list to the points that, in your gut, you feel are more important
- make a pros column and cons column for each point

- work through each point, and at the end decide whether it's more of a pro or a con
- count out the pros and cons – by this stage, regardless of the actual number of pro/cons, you will probably have put enough thought into it to make an informed decision.

This activity serves three main purposes:

1. The pro/con chart is an exercise in detachment.
2. If you feel confident in your decision, don't spend time ruminating over it. This frees up your mind for positive thoughts.
3. If you have genuinely thought it over, and are sure about the decision you came to, stay strong when letting them know (if your answer is negative). You don't necessarily have to explain why – just stick to your decision. The other inmate will respect you for standing your ground.

Repetitive positive thinking

The environmental stimuli around inmates with ASD can be overwhelming:

- lighting
- echo-prone units
- boisterous people
- crowding.

A handy technique to help subdue the impact of these stimuli is to use repetitive thinking – a positive thought, said over and over in your mind, like a mantra. You can have different mantras for different types of moods, but always keep the mantra positive.

Repeating 'I wish that CO was dead' again and again is *not* a good coping mechanism. Reminding yourself you will be going home one day, and every *second* that goes by brings you closer, *is* a good coping mechanism.

Mindfulness

The most aggressive, alpha male-orientated unit I was in taught me, through necessity, how to use mindfulness as a coping mechanism. At first, I didn't even realise I was practising it, until I explained to a friend what I was doing, and why, and he told me it was in fact mindfulness I was engaging in.

I first recognised it in the yard. It would be post-workout (I always trained as early as was reasonable – about 9.00 am till 10.00 am), and I would still be feeling the release of endorphins. I'd bring a book out with me and find a sunny spot to just sit and read. Sometimes I would be interrupted, either deliberately or by sudden loud noises. When this happened, I began to focus on my breathing, the sunlight on my skin, the way the book felt in my hands and the breeze on my face. Then I'd go through a list of things I was grateful for, right then and there: I had eaten, I had exercised, I had a book to read and nobody was giving me a hard time. After that, I'd think about the bigger picture of gratefulness: my gratitude to my loving family, my friends, gratitude I wasn't doing time in Siberia or North Korea, that I was... alive. More than alive. I was alive and making the most of my situation.

From then on, I made a point of practising mindfulness, even when I got into the SNU and things were so much quieter.

Mindfulness is not a tricky or complex cognitive strategy. It's a matter of:

- focusing on the positive
- being grateful for what you have
- blocking out/ignoring (as best you can) negative stimuli
- living in the moment.

Some inmates spend time focusing on what they *don't* have, rather than what they *do*. Make a point of watching the news, especially the world news if you can. It will help put things in perspective. *Somewhere, someone always has it worse than you.* If negativity starts to spread through your thoughts like poison gas, put on your mindfulness mask. It might not eliminate the poisonous thoughts, but it will dilute them.

Compartmentalise the day

This is especially relevant if you are confined to a cell for long periods, such as being in the DU or if there's a measles outbreak and the whole facility is locked down. If you find yourself in this situation, it's important you try to break the day into hours, and have set things you do, even if it's just reading, or working out, or showering, or napping. Always keep routine up, even in solitary.

Mental Detachment

This is like meditation, so try it in your cell first. It can be done outside your cell, but there may be distractions.

- Close your eyes.
- Focus on an imaginary 'inner spot' in your brain.

- Focus on your breathing.
- Take deep breaths in, hold for five seconds, and breathe out slowly.
- Repeat.

This will slow your mind. Physiologically, slowing your breathing slows your heart rate. Mentally, it gives a sense of clarity and peace. You could try it right now, and you'll see the difference.

Narrative-based therapy

If you have associated with Alcoholics or Narcotics Anonymous (AA or NA), this will sound familiar – it's the fundamental premise behind these organisations. It's a method where you talk out loud about your life, your struggles up to the current point in time and what you think you can do to help make better choices. This is done in front of a group in AA/NA. And as anyone who has attended meetings can confirm, some regular attendees repeat the same story, regardless of how many times they've told it before.

These people are using narrative-based therapy to stay sober/clean. They play the well-worn tape in their mind, speak it out loud and come to the same conclusion again: 'My life is better without drugs and/or alcohol.'

Irrespective of whether you have an alcohol or drug problem, this type of therapy can help you cope while locked up. Tell your life story (to yourself), quietly but out loud, so you are essentially mapping all the significant points of your life. This will help you become confident about who you are and put jail into perspective. That is, it will remind you jail is a *chapter* in your life story, *not* the overriding theme.

Finally

Methods inmates use to cope in jail are as varied as the inmates themselves. There is no surefire fix for problems you might encounter. Just remember:

- Live and let live.
- See no evil, hear no evil, speak no evil.
- Watch, listen and learn.
- Stand your ground.

People with ASD are often strong, stubborn people, and there are those of us who have been to jail and walked out of the gates stronger, wiser, more patient and more confident. Aim to make this you.

CHAPTER 18

Pre-Jail, Post-Jail

Introduction

It may seem odd to include a 'pre-jail' section at the very *end* of the book. It's included because the advice given will make more sense after you have digested the preceding text. It's a misconception that once your sentence (including parole) is finished, you are free. While technically no longer behind bars, you may be dragging around a metaphorical ball and chain comprising pent-up resentment, anger, frustration and self-doubt. This weight, if not addressed, has the potential to drag you under. What you don't want to become is another cynical, bitter ex-con.

Please note
There is no one-size-fits-all approach to re-entering society. How you cope is very individualistic. However, there is one piece of advice that is applicable to all jail-leavers – aim to develop a strong support network.

Pre-Jail

There are measures you can take to maximise your confidence prior to going inside. Obviously, this is applicable to people who have been charged, granted bail and are awaiting trial. Or you've been granted bail but want to cover all bases in case it's a guilty verdict. This can give you up to six months (possibly more with adjournments) to prepare for possible incarceration.

Measures you can take
Talk to ex-prisoners:

My father met a man who has ASD and had broken the law. He was facing possible jail time. He wasn't naturally a criminal, he wasn't a drug user, he wasn't a trained fighter. In other words, he was in for a rough time (potentially, anyway – anyone can find the inner strength to rise above the bullshit in jail – though they might not believe it yet). So Dad asked me if I would talk to him. He was very interested in what I had to say, and he told me I had helped allay his fears significantly.

Luckily, he was given a suspended sentence, so he never had to face jail, but it's a good example of how talking to an ex-prisoner can be a source of comfort and strength. He would ring me at odd hours, which I had insisted he do if his thoughts became too loud and worrying. He later told me I had 'been a huge source of comfort'. That meant a lot to me. All I want to do is help people – give them an ear to talk to, a shoulder to cry on or a torch to light the way through the darkness. I've been through a fair share of shit in my life, and now I want to help others avoid making some of the mistakes I did.

Talking to an ex-prisoner may take some legwork. If you are struggling with drugs, you could attend NA meetings and explain your position during a 'share', and almost certainly someone there will have done time, and would be willing to help you. You could also:

- Try looking up prisoner support groups on the internet.
- If you can't find a *prisoner* support group, enquire about the equivalent for parents/family of prisoners – they will be able to point you in the right direction.
- If you have a therapist, perhaps they might know how to help you find a prisoner to talk to. Any ex-prisoner who is willing to give up their time to help others is going to be amenable.
- Religious groups may know ex-prisoners who found solace in religion, so you could try different religious groups.

Contact mental health services in advance

While I was in the Bronx, the crappiest unit of them all, I was struggling to be put on my diazepam (as mentioned in a personal anecdote earlier in the book). My mother did all she could to help, which included being able to ascertain, through the internet and polite phone calls, how to contact the person who oversaw mental health services for the state's prisons.

She spoke with this doctor, and that gave me great relief – Mum had gone over the gatekeepers and straight to the source. It was a comfort. He wrote to my mother, explaining the problems the jail system faced dealing with mental health issues, due mostly to lack of funding and lack of compassion from those who hold the purse strings. But knowing someone had spoken to the head honcho on my behalf was a great comfort. And if you can do it before incarceration, all the better.

The prisons in a certain state/territory/precinct will be governed by the same body, so contacting them regarding your ASD will cover you for remand, reception and placement jails. You can kill three birds with one stone. By alerting the mental health team that oversees the prisons in your jurisdiction, you may be able to move straight into the SNU (or equivalent) when you get transported from the watch house to remand jail.

Avoid prison stimuli

As simple as it sounds, try to minimise exposure to movies, fictional books, TV shows or documentaries about jail. Most of these mediums are either outright wrong or, in the case of documentaries, sensationalised.

Work out

Developing an exercise routine before going inside serves three main purposes:

1. It will make you feel good and relaxed (all exercise does).
2. It will increase your size.
3. Inmates do respect other inmates for working out – it shows discipline.

Remember to focus on calisthenics (using your own body weight as resistance), because there won't be much exercise equipment in the jail yards.

Martial arts

There are classes you can take to learn a few basic but effective techniques that can minimise the risk of getting hurt. Obviously, four to six months isn't enough time to become Bruce Lee, but it is enough time to learn the fundamentals of self-defence.

The focus is on self-defence, not learning how to bash someone's brain in. Another advantage is it will give you an inner confidence, which inmates will pick up on. Taking these classes will allow you to become familiar with the feeling of being near someone who wants to hurt you, but without the fear. Over time, as you become more familiar with self-defence, the fear will reduce.

Please note
Do *not* tell people you have taken these classes, lest someone wants to 'test' your skill level.

Haircut
Most male inmates have shaved heads. This is for three reasons:

- It's easy to maintain.
- It looks 'tough'.
- If you are in a fight, being able to grab your opponent's hair can give you a distinct advantage.

So, if you have a 'style cut', consider shaving it off prior to jail (or use the communal clippers once you get to jail). Remember, hair grows back.

Post-Jail

While staring through the bars of the yard, looking at the same view you have had for the last 700 days, it's natural to assume that, once released, it's all over and done with. That it was no more than a 'phase' you endured and it can now be put upon a shelf in the recesses of your mind. Frustratingly, this isn't the case. Jail doesn't let go that easily. It's like the frustrating ex-partner who keeps popping up when you least need them.

When my second parole finally came through, and I was able to escape the Bronx unit at placement jail, I was obviously relieved. However, even though I was technically free, I was still on parole, so I didn't feel free. Looking back, I think I was more stressed than I realised.

When released, they gave me five days' worth of medication, along with about AUS$500 (which is a loan, not a gift). I had only just been put on diazepam (after fighting the system for three and a half months to get it), so when I took all 15 tablets, it rocked me. By 4.00 pm, I had been free for six hours, and had bought 400 mg of morphine, and $100 worth of speed (on top of the diazepam). This 'binge' didn't last more than 48 hours, but I had thought getting out from that shithole would have been euphoric enough. Apparently, it wasn't. My psychiatrist, who has known me a long time, suggested my behaviour stemmed from pent-up anxiety, akin to a stressed employee having a couple of beers after work – except my behaviour was a turbo-charged version of the concept.

Another concept my psychiatrist suggested is that I may have been suffering from low-level post-traumatic stress disorder (PTSD). He explained that because of my ASD, I had to be hypervigilant for ten hours a day (7.00 am–5.00 pm), seven days a week. Without my diazepam to help me cope with my ASD-induced social worries, PTSD was a likely ramification (luckily, it was low-level PTSD).

PTSD

PTSD is very real and can have its roots in prolonged negative experiences (war, jail, domestic violence, bullying, etc.) or quick, intense negative experiences (road traffic accidents, acts of terrorism, being involved in a robbery, etc.). Symptoms of PTSD vary between individuals, but can include:

- distressing/intrusive memories of event(s) (e.g. flashbacks, nightmares)
- finding ways to avoid memories (e.g. drugs, alcohol, gambling)
- an inability to experience positive emotions (e.g. depressive episodes, and a lack of interest in previously enjoyable activities).

There's no surefire method to help someone with PTSD attributed to jail. Seeking professional help sooner rather than later is important, as is avoiding 'triggers' of unwanted memories, such as shows or documentaries about prison, or even talk about prison. People will be curious, so be ready for that. Only tell them small amounts. Don't just say, 'I don't want to talk about it', because people will assume you were the victim of a sexual assault, and you *do not* want idiots whispering that kind of nonsense about you.

Parole

Unless you decide to do your whole sentence from start to finish (which is very rare), you will be dealing with probation and parole. Your assigned parole officer (PO) will explain clearly what is expected of you. Prior to being released, a CO will have given you details of where, when and to whom you must report after walking out the gates. Generally, you have 24–48 hours to contact your PO. *Even if your PO is difficult, rise above it. You don't want them to develop a dislike of you – they can make your life difficult should they choose.*

Urine tests (again)

You may be asked to provide a UT while on parole. This is not a given – it will depend on:

- where you are (jurisdiction)
- your crime
- your parole conditions
- your PO.

As mentioned earlier, shy bladder syndrome (or paruresis) is more common than people think. As with the jail authorities, let your PO know as soon as possible about this with letters from your psychiatrist, GP or psychologist. *Annoyingly, failure to produce a sample is counted as a negative result, or 'dirty'.* That's why addressing shy bladder syndrome is very important.

I suffer from shy bladder syndrome, and it proved to be an awkward foible for parole (as well as in jail). If I knew I had a parole appointment at a certain time, I would start drinking water in large amounts about 90 minutes before I was due to go. If you drink enough, you can produce a sample every 25 minutes or so, giving you ample leeway. Plus, I had my psychiatrist's backing and I was always polite, so there was never a big problem with UTs.

Don't stagnate

Do something constructive with your time. If you have a predilection towards drugs or alcohol, this is especially important.

Work

Work is probably the best option. If you're under 40, genuinely committed to finding work and are open-minded, something will come up. This isn't a book about finding employment. However, anecdotally, it seems those who get jobs quickly after release almost always fare well.

Study

Study is a plausible option, especially if you went into jail as an addict and got clean. Your brain will be clear, and you're used to strong routine, boundaries and self-discipline – precisely the qualities conducive to study.

Volunteering

If you are having trouble landing a job, and don't feel like studying, there's the option of volunteering. Many people with ASD love animals – perhaps investigate a volunteering role involving animals.

Whatever you do, don't sit around watching TV all day. If you were working out in jail, keep working out on the outside. If you kept a journal while inside, keep writing while at home. Routine is the backbone of healthy functioning.

Smell the roses

Obviously, one will appreciate freedom and see the world in a slightly different light after being released. What's not expected is just how fast ex-prisoners can lose their appreciation of freedom. Wake up each day and count your blessings: you can travel far and wide; no one's going to get in your face unless you start trouble. Appreciate the comparatively lightning fast access to medical treatment.

Roses lose their scent over time. It's the natural order of things. But even when a flower is no longer fragrant, your memory of its sweetness can linger forever.

The long arm of the law

> *I had been out about three days. I was walking to the train station and an unmarked police car pulled into the driveway I was about to cross. It wasn't a dangerous manoeuvre, but it did surprise me.*
>
> *'Mr Attwood,' the driver said pleasantly, 'how was prison?'*
>
> *I recognised him as one of the detectives who had raided my unit three years before.*
>
> *'Fine,' I smiled. There was a pause.*
>
> *'Well,' he said, putting the car into reverse, 'stay out of trouble.'*
>
> *'Will do.' I said. I haven't seen him since.*

The point is the local police will get a 'heads up' when a prisoner is getting released into their territory. So don't go and do anything stupid, because they may be keeping an eye on you.

Sorry, it's on a need-to-know basis

Lastly, choose carefully whom you tell about your incarceration. Obviously, your family and close friends will already know, and by proxy some peripheral people. What's more important is how you approach the issue of divulging your prison time to other people. *If you land a job, and make a friend, don't assume that just because they seem reliable they can keep their mouth shut.* Never underestimate people's ability to:

- not keep a secret
- revel in gossip
- lack compassion
- fail to even *try* hearing the other side of the story
- fail to show sympathy/empathy.

It took months, and dozens of applications, but I eventually got a part-time job. I got it through an agency that, in part, specialises in helping people find employment regardless of time spent in jail, so I figured my boss knew I'd done time. Still, I kept my mouth shut.

I befriended a nice, naïve young woman whom I felt I could trust, and it turns out I could. I told her about jail, and she was good to her word – she kept it to herself. One day I was telling her some little story about my time inside, and neither of us had realised it, but a fellow employee had slipped in the side door and heard every word.

Within a fortnight I was out of a job. Apparently, the parents of some of the young women I worked with had said they didn't want their 'young' (20- to 25-year-old) daughters working 'with a criminal'. Even though my crime involved no violence or sexual component (nor does my entire rap sheet), they saw me as a threat and the boss had to fire me, or risk losing a third of his workforce overnight. He was very apologetic, and I bear him no grudge. I never bothered to 'get revenge' or anything silly like that; I just left it alone.

I included this story to illustrate how people often have knee-jerk reactions to 'criminals', and they don't even want to know the details – it's safer and easier for them to see criminals as some strange entity, a blemish on society. To think of them as someone's son, daughter, brother, sister – that would require them to ask some hard questions they don't want to think about, like, 'What if that were my son who I'd just picked up from jail? Could I really act like he didn't exist, give him the cold shoulder and walk away?' They know they couldn't. So they avoid all but skimming the surface of these tougher conundrums.

A Final Word

If you've read this far, you will have developed a decent insight into jail and, more specifically, jail for those with ASD. But no matter how many movies (which are mostly inaccurate anyway) or documentaries (which are heavily edited to create the atmosphere the producers want the audience to see, which is drama and tension) you watch, or books you read (everyone has a different experience), there is no tried-and-tested way to prepare anyone for jail. This book can only take you so far, and can only answer broader, more generalised questions. But this is an accurate depiction of life in a maximum security prison – nothing has been downplayed, nothing has been embellished. More specifically, this book will help you understand how jail can be for those with ASD.

Hopefully, with time, education and awareness programs, inmates with ASD will be treated as they are now being treated in progressive schools – where the focus is still on learning, but the staff understand the idiosyncrasies of each student with ASD and can take measures to minimise emotional distress. In school, emotional distress may result in class disruption. In jail, emotional distress may result in violence or suicide.

The sooner the judicial systems address the needs of inmates with ASD, the sooner we can truly say we live in a society where the essence of incarceration is the deprivation of freedom, not whether any given law-breaker can 'handle jail'. All inmates are entitled to feel safe and supported – not scared and sad, with no one to turn to within the system itself for help. Deprivation of liberty is the punishment, not deprivation of dignity.

Hopefully, this book will go some distance to closing the gap between the haves and have-nots behind the razor wire; after all, every prisoner is doing it hard. A system that identifies and accommodates vulnerable inmates should be considered standard, not progressive. But until that day comes, there are people out there who care, who want to make a difference. There are people who want inmates with ASD to come out of jail feeling wiser for the experience, instead of emerging as another broken soul one step from falling between the societal cracks of recidivism. It's a team effort – with luck this book will contribute to a culture where it's freedom prisoners are deprived of, not their sense of security or happiness.

Glossary

ASD Autism spectrum disorder. Asperger's syndrome is also known as ASD Level 1.

Aspie A colloquial term to describe somebody diagnosed with Asperger's syndrome.

Bail Can mean one of two things: (a) Someone is charged with a crime, and they apply for *bail* instead of waiting in jail until their trial or sentencing; (b) An inmate '*bails*' from a unit while in prison. This means they have been threatened with violence if they do not voluntarily leave the unit. This may be for any number of reasons, such as they are suspected of being a prison informant.

Big House A slang term for prison.

Breaches Refers to being 'breached' while in jail. This is an in-jail punishment and can happen for several reasons; punishments vary from a warning to time in the detention unit.

'Bronx' units Units considered by inmates to be particularly dangerous and/or where it is difficult to get enough food and basics such as sugar. Basically, a unit with a lot of alpha males.

Buy-up Also known as 'canteen', buy-up is the weekly process of filling in a form to choose from a limited but decent amount of grocery items that will be paid for from your prison account and arrive on the same day each week.

Cellie Cellmate. The person with whom you share a cell.

Cheeseballing   When an inmate becomes too 'familiar' with the COs, or spends more time interacting with them than is necessary, or they smile and act like friends. As in 'Look at so-and-so, cheeseballing with the screws. He better knock it off before someone teaches him a lesson.'

CO or (COs)   Correctional (or corrections) officer. The employees who staff jails.

Dogging   Seemingly exclusive to Australia, this term refers to the act of providing police (or any authority) with information regarding the actions of other people, illegal or otherwise. It's an adult's way of saying 'dobbing' or 'telling on someone'.

Dope sickness   Refers to the unpleasant physical and mental symptoms an addict experiences when abrupt cessation of their drug occurs, such as a heroin addict suddenly cut off from all supplies. This is seen in the early days of incarceration.

Doubled-up   If you are 'doubled-up', this means you will be sharing a cell at night with another inmate.

Down-low   Means to keep something secret, or at least not make it widely known. For example, if you have access to medications other inmates might want, keep that information on the down-low, lest they find out and pester or threaten you for the medication.

Drug diverting   The practice of an inmate creating the illusion they have swallowed their pills when in fact they have pushed them to the corner of their mouths, to be retrieved later for selling, swapping or stockpiling.

DU   Short for detention unit, this is where inmates are sent for punishment. Like a 'jail within a jail', conditions are sparse and it's uncomfortable – hence it being used for punishment.

DVO   Acronym for domestic violence order, a form of restraining order designed to keep people safe from people they don't want to see. This term applies only to the outside world. You cannot take out a DVO against someone in jail or take one out on someone from inside jail.

Facing time   Means somebody is expecting to go to jail for something they did. They may have been granted bail but are pretty sure they will end up pleading guilty and are therefore 'facing time'.

Fish bowl   A term used in some jails to refer to the area where the COs sit and observe the unit. From here they can access computer info (such as an inmate's account balance), distribute mail and so on.

'Getting the skinny'   Finding out information about an event or person or something of interest, usually from a friend. As in 'I got the skinny about why they had a fight from my cellmate.'

Headcount   The process of making sure all inmates are accounted for.

Heads up   This means someone is giving you information that is of some value and/or helpful. For example, 'Hey mate, just giving you the heads up, the screws just busted a whole lot of dudes in such-and-such a unit, and I think they might be comin' here next, so be careful.'

Lackey   Usually used in the sense of you *don't* want to be anyone's lackey (a person who does exactly what's asked of them without question), *especially* not a CO's lackey.

Lifer   An inmate who has been sentenced to life and has either spent a long time inside or *will* be spending a long time inside.

Lockdown   This is when all inmates are expected to go to their cells to be 'locked down' for the evening. Lockdowns can also happen for other reasons, such as staff training or a medical emergency.

Lollies (sweets, candy)   Sweet, sugary treats available on buy-up (canteen).

Mainstream   There are two 'tiers' of jail – mainstream and protection. Protection is designed for vulnerable inmates, such as those who have hurt a child, and are therefore at risk of physical harm from fellow inmates. Mainstream is for criminals who have committed crimes considered 'acceptable' by fellow inmates.

Mindfulness   The art of 'living in the moment', as opposed to worrying about the future or dwelling on the past.

Movement   As in 'prisoner movement'. This is used to refer to the practice of the jail only moving one tier of inmates at a time. For example, if you're in mainstream, you may have to wait for the walkways to be clear of protection inmates before being allowed to move around the jail (such as to a class, medical, the oval, visits, etc.).

Muster   The assembly of inmates, either by their cell doors or lined up around the yard perimeter, to ensure all are accounted for. The prelude to the 'headcount'.

Medical   An all-encompassing term for the building that involves physical health, mental health, the distribution point for medications considered too risky to give to inmates in their units (such as morphine, steroids or insulin), and where people who have been injured come to be checked out.

Old mate   A term used to describe an individual whose name you don't know but to whom your feelings are neutral. For example: 'Look at old mate over there – he definitely knows what he's doing when it comes to exercise.'

'On the spectrum'   As it sounds, this refers to an individual who is on the autism spectrum.

Outside charge   While incarcerated, most incidents are dealt with 'in-house' – for example, an inmate is given some time in the DU for fighting or being caught with a medication that isn't theirs. However, some incidents are serious enough to warrant the police getting involved, such as a jail murder or when an inmate assaults a CO. In cases like these, the inmate will face an 'outside charge' in a court, and this may add time to their sentence.

Oval/gym   Used together because, more often than not, the facilities are adjacent to each other. So, you won't go to one without going to the other.

Parole breaches   These occur when an individual on parole fails to meet one of the conditions upon which they were released – for example, failing to be at home at 11.00 pm when a 7.00 pm to 7.00 am curfew was one of the conditions. Parole breaches often result in a return to incarceration.

PO   Parole officer. When you get out on parole, as the vast majority of inmates do, you will be assigned a parole officer, or PO.

Politics   Politics is a generic term used to describe any gossip, rumours or Chinese whispers that are going around. It can also refer to the drug scene, as in 'The drug scene is fraught with politics'.

p.r.n.   Latin for *'pro re nata'* meaning 'as needed'. This term is used for medications. Aspirin is an example of a medication administered p.r.n.

'Punch-on'   This refers to two inmates fighting, as in 'I think those two guys are about to have a punch-on'.

Ramped   When a cell/cells/entire unit is searched for contraband, this is known as ramping. Sometimes units are frequently ramped, sometimes months will pass between cell searches.

'Run-of-the-mill units'   One step down from Bronx units, these aren't considered particularly easy to live in, but they're not considered as tough as the Bronx units.

Screws   The most well-known and commonly used word to describe a CO. Although not *technically* an insult, COs prefer to be called COs.

Singled-out   The opposite of being doubled-up; that is, you will have a cell to yourself.

SNU   The special needs unit is a unit that caters for inmates who for one reason or another simply aren't coping in the normal units. There's less violence and a more relaxed atmosphere.

Solitary   Refers to the practice of locking a prisoner into a cell for 22 or 23 hours a day. Some inmates are in solitary in the form of the DU (detention unit), while others are kept in solitary in medical (where the conditions aren't as sparse) because they simply cannot safely interact with other inmates, but the authorities don't want to deprive them of 'luxuries' such as TV as they do in the DU, because they aren't there to be punished.

Teller   This is an inmate who isn't a dog (informant) but has said something innocuous to a CO and another inmate thinks they are untrustworthy because of it. Usually these inmates (who think someone is a 'teller') are paranoid gossips.

Turtles   This term refers to the correctional officers who deal with violent/uncooperative inmates. They're called this because they can use their shields to form a 'shell-like' group entity and move through groups of rioting inmates. They look like special operations police without weapons.

Your people   A term used to encapsulate all the people on the outside with whom you communicate.

Index

Aboriginals 129, 186
acquired brain injuries (ABIs) 66
Alcoholics Anonymous (AA) 277
alpha males 68, 199, 203, 215, 241, 254, 275
American jails 186, 211
analgesia 92, 93, 122, 284
antidepressants 122, 266
antipsychotics 96, 121
anxiety management 97
armed robbery 19, 29, 33, 85
arrival in jail 74–86
　buy-ups 77
　change, expecting 80
　dietary requirements 37, 78
　first impressions 43, 79–80
　flexibility and routine 80
　medical processing 78
　moral compass, arbitrary 82–3
　prison number and PIN 77–8
　processing, final part 76–7
　reasons for incarceration, asking about 82
　reception call 79
　social aspects 79
　tips to help newcomer 84–6
　what to expect 74–6
ASD see autism spectrum disorder (ASD)
assaults 90
　on COs 238–9
　on police officers 30

Australian jails 11, 77, 129, 158, 185–6, 211
　see also Aboriginals
autism spectrum disorder (ASD), inmates with
　addiction 35
　ASD-specific issues 40–1, 93
　and boredom 125–6
　and change 88
　divulging of diagnosis 18, 39–40, 62–71
　　argument against telling corrective services 65–7
　　as back-up plan 67
　　to COs 80
　　decision-making 64–5, 67–71
　drug-related issues 114–15
　eye contact 84
　group-based learning 137
　hypersensitivity 40
　medical needs 93
　nervousness 249–50
　SNU, going to 62, 63–4
　special interests (SIs) 125–6, 130, 252, 260–1
　watch house/holding cells 34–5

bail 17, 67, 70, 222, 280
　applying for 26, 28
　'bailers' 64
behavioural conduct 41
benzodiazepines 39, 45, 92, 93, 96, 97, 101, 106, 121, 122, 284

bipolar disorder 66
body searches 36–7, 75
boredom 125–6, 146
bowel movements 192, 196
brain damage 66
breaches 53, 121, 160, 205
　and correctional officers 232–3
　parole 45, 116, 129
Bronx (tough) units 69, 174, 182, 258, 281, 284
bullying/harassment 32, 68, 69, 109, 205–6, 207, 258
　and social interaction 223–4
buprenorphine 115
bureaucracy, jail 150
bus, prison 57–8
busy, keeping see keeping busy
buy-ups (ordering of grocery items) 76–7, 154–5
　social interaction 206–7

cameras 173, 244
canines 171–2
canteens see buy-ups (ordering of grocery items)
cards 131, 132, 218
cavity searches 37, 116
celebrities 32
cellie 199, 200, 202, 203
change 80, 88
cheeseballing (being 'familiar' with COs) 235
children
　avoiding topic of 188–9
　offences against 31, 33, 83, 188
cleanliness 200–1
clothing 75, 165–6

collective
punishment 214, 232, 238
communication
  conciliatory gestures/
    language 254–6
  with COs 231
  different jails 252–3
  hot-button topics 251–2
  keeping cool if
    confronted 251
  nervousness 249–50
  neutral, guidelines
    for 246–9
  non-verbal 253–6
  physical 254
  verbal 245–53
community service 27
compartment-
alisation 276
compassion 39, 94, 98,
203, 256, 269, 281
confessions 26
confrontation,
avoiding 241–58
  being challenged,
    coping with 256–7
  drug rehabilitation
    units 242
  'engineering' a safer
    environment 242–3
  in-unit
    precautions 243
  keeping cool if
    confronted 251
  non-verbal comm-
    unication 253–6
  outside unit
    precautions 243–4
  special needs units
    (SNUs) 242–3
  verbal comm-
    unication 245–53
  ways to 'hide' 244–5
  workers units 242
contraband see
ramping (searching for
contraband)

coping mechanisms 259–78
  being challenged 256–7
  compart-
    mentalisation 276
  counting one's
    blessings 272
  curiosity and
    compassion 269
  diet and exercise 264
  drawing 261
  intellectual
    development 262
  mental strategies 273–7
  mindfulness 275–6
  music 261–2, 271
  narrative-based
    therapy 277
  negative thinking,
    minimising 269–72,
    276
  outside world,
    maintaining contact
    with 269–70
  physical
    approach 263–6
  practical action 259–63
  professionals, talking
    to 262–3
  repetitive positive
    thinking 274–5
  sanctuaries,
    finding 261
  singling-out,
    ensuring 259–60
  sleep 265–6
  social interaction 266
  solution-based therapy
    (SBT) 273–4
  special interests
    (SIs) 125–6, 260–1
  sunlight 266
  television 270–1
  warm thoughts 271–2
  writing 261
  yoga 265
correctional
departments 57, 97
correctional facilities 17,
28, 46, 57, 95, 128, 129, 172

correctional officers
(COs) 30, 53, 64,68,
78–80, 134, 148–150, 167,
186, 193, 211, 217, 231, 232,
255, 267
  assaulting 238–9
  and breaches 160,
    232–3
  conversing with 234–5
  and drugs 114, 121
  and fighting 70–1,
    90–1, 236–8
  fine line 235–6
  headcounts 107, 108
  interacting with 230–40
  keeping quiet
    about 239–40
  and medical needs 90,
    98, 99, 106
  power-hungry 267–9
  and receiving
    mail 153–4
  riot squads 170–1
  and transport 58, 61
  unlocking by 103, 104
  and urine tests 163–4,
    233–4
  and visits 156, 157
  weekly
    inspections 168–9
  see also fish bowl
    (COs' offices); turtles
    (correction officers
    dealing with violent
    inmates)
creative writing 143–4
curiosity 269
custodial and non-
custodial sentences 27

debt 32, 209
detention for purposes of
questioning 23–4
detention units
(DUs) 104–5, 121, 160,
233, 247, 276
  assaults on COs 238,
    239

reasons for DU
time 161
and solitary
confinement 161–3
diazepam (Valium) 39,
45, 92, 93, 101, 115, 121, 122,
123, 284
see also benzo-
diazepines
dietary requirements 37,
78, 109
disease control 175
DNA 37
dogging (providing police
with information) 53, 70
dogs 171–2
domestic violence orders
(DVOs) 20
dope sickness 45
doubling-up (sharing
a cell with another
inmate) 55, 173, 174,
193–6, 198–200, 202, 203,
227, 260, 267
see also sharing a cell;
singling-out (having
cell to oneself)
down-low (keeping
something secret) 256
drawing 144, 261
drug diverting 106
defining 121
drugs in demand 121–3
taking other people's
diverted meds 123
drugs 114–24
addiction 35, 85, 92,
120
and ASD 114–15
coming into jail from
outside 116, 117–20
price 118
safety issues 119–20
and stress 118–19
dope sickness 45
driving under
influence of 60
'drug corner' 120
drug rehabilitation
units 242

drug-seeking
behaviour 92–3
inside use 123–4
intravenous 120
placement jails 117
reasons for using 117
reception jails 51
remand jails 50, 116
street drugs 115, 117
subgroups 115
swaps 207–8
types 116–17
urine tests *see* urine
tests (UTs)
withdrawal from 40, 43
see also drug diverting;
medications
DUs *see* detention units
(DUs)
DVOs *see* domestic
violence orders (DVOs)

educational courses
access to
education 159–60
ASD and group-based
learning 137
and group
activities 133–8
learning on one's
own 139–40
placement jails 135,
136–7
post-jail 287
reception jails 133
remand jails 133–4
empathy 94
everyday life 102–13
afternoon medications
(approx 4.00
pm) 110–11
breakfast (7.00–9.00
am) 105–6
dinner (4.30 pm) 111
first access (9.00–10.30
am) 107
headcounts (at
10.30 am and 2.30
pm) 107–9, 110

lockdown (5.00
pm) 111–12
lunch (12–1 pm) 109
morning medication
(approx 8.00 am) 106–
7
night time 112–13
second access (1.00–
2.30 pm) 109–10
unlocking (opening
of cells around 7.30
am) 103–5, 111, 164
evidence, impossible to
refute 26–7
exercise
coping
mechanisms 264
etiquette 210
in groups 132
martial arts 282–3
as natural anti-
depressant 264
on one's own 139
working out 132,
209–12, 282
expertise 252
eye contact 84, 253, 255

facing time 20–1, 220, 256
fighting 54, 57, 215,
218–20
and correctional
officers (COs) 70–1,
90–1, 236–8
fingerprints 37
first impressions 43,
79–80
first names 192–3
first-timers' unit, unit
and cell allocation 148
fish bowl (COs'
offices) 211
flatulence 192, 196
fluoxetine 266
frustration 94, 143, 202

gambling 131, 209
games 131–2, 218
general manager (GM),
writing to 98–9

going home
etiquette 220–1
gratitude 272
group activities 133–8
    ASD and group-based
        learning 137
    oval/gym time 137–8
    placement jails 136
    reception jails 133,
        134–5
    remand jails 133–4
group showers 166
guilt, admitting 27, 28

handcuffs 58, 100
harassment see bullying/
    harassment
headcounts 154, 192, 235
    everyday life 104,
        107–9, 107–10, 110
heads up 288
health
    mental see mental
        health
    physical 90–3, 94
helping people 140–1
Hepatitis C 119
high-profilers 32, 175
HIV 119
holding cells see watch
    house/holding cells
hope 256
hospitals 91–2
hot-button topics 251–2
hunger strikes 109
hypersensitivity, in
    ASD 40

ID cards 75, 89, 107, 111,
    149, 156
ideological clashes 201–2
induction unit, unit and
    cell allocation 148
in-house induction 148
injuries, avoiding 90
innocent prisoners 25–6
inspections, weekly 168–
    9, 201
intelligence 141, 142

intensive correction
    order (ICO) 27
intercoms 174
interviews 24–7
    handling 25–7
    practical issues 24–5
    intimate contact and
        body exposure 225–8
    in-unit precautions 243
    involuntary treatment
        order (ITO) 100

jailhouse informants 32
jails 47–56
    arrival 74–86
    Australian 11, 58, 77,
        129, 185–6, 211
    communication
        in 252–3
    differences 18, 252–3
    navigating 176–7
    placement see
        placement jails
    pragmatic
        aspects 147–80
    prisoners, types
        of 47–8
    reasons for
        incarceration 21, 82
    reception see reception
        jails
    remand see remand
        jails
    similarities 11
    time spent in, effect 28
    types 48–9

keeping busy 125–46
    being active during the
        day 130–1
    constructive use of
        time 126–7
    educational courses
        and group
        activities 133–8
    friendships,
        forming 128–30
    helping people 140–1
    social activities 131–3

social vs. solo
    activities 127–8
    time alone 138–46
King, Stephen 220

laundry 165, 217
learning difficulties 66
legal documents 170
legal representatives 24,
    26, 28
library 149
lifers 217, 232, 241
lights out 199
listening 94, 110, 190, 243,
    246, 270
    to conversations 247,
        269
    to music 189, 262
    and watching/
        learning 44, 143, 206
lockdowns 50, 104, 107,
    172, 268
    assaults on COs 238,
        239
    everyday life 111–13
    reasons for 174–6

mail, sending and
    receiving 153–4
mainstream inmates
    children, avoiding
        topic of 188, 189
    and watch house 31, 32
    see also protected
        inmates
martial arts 282–3
masturbation 197–8
medical emergencies 174
medical needs 87–101
    ASD-specific issues 93
    drug-seeking
        behaviour 92–3
    issues beyond scope of
        jail 91–2
    mental health 93–101
    physical health 90–3
    placement jails 88–9
    processing 78
    reception jails 51–2, 88
    remand jails 88

INDEX

watch house/holding
cells 38–40
see also medications
medical ombudsman 99
medications 38–40
afternoon (approx 4.00
pm) 110–11
anti-anxiety 97
antidepressants 122,
266
antipsychotics 96, 121
benzodiazepines 39,
45, 92, 93, 96, 97, 101,
106, 121, 122
methadone 45, 101
morning (approx 8.00
am) 106–7
painkillers 92, 93, 122,
284
p.r.n. (*pro re nata*) (as
needed) 93
watch house/holding
cells 38–40
see also drugs
mental detachment 276–7
mental health 93–101
compromise, life as 98
contacting mental
health services in
advance 281–2
dissatisfaction with
care 98–9
potential vicious
cycle 94–5
psychiatric expert,
seeing 87, 95–8
reaching out 95
mental health team 260,
262
mental strategies
compart-
mentalisation 276
detachment 273, 276–7
mindfulness 275–6
narrative-based
therapy 277
reading 273
repetitive positive
thinking 274–5
solution-based therapy
(SBT) 273–4

methadone 45, 101
mimicking 42, 81
mindfulness 275–6
miscarriages of justice 25
'model prisoner' 135
morphine 92, 284
movement of
prisoners 32–3, 48, 49,
52–5, 64, 175, 203
movies 187–8
mugshots 37
music 189–90, 202
coping
mechanisms 261–2,
271
muster (assembly of
inmates) 104, 108, 268

Narcotics Anonymous
(NA) 277
narrative-based
therapy 277
navigating the jail 176–7
negative thinking,
minimising 269–72, 276
neuropathic pain, drugs
for 122
neurotransmitters 266
noise 40
nurse care 39

olanzapine (Zyprexa) 96
old mate 61, 71
outside charges 176, 238
outside unit
precautions 243–4
outside world,
maintaining contact
with 269–70
oval/gym time 55, 137–8
overcrowding 195, 260
oxycodone 92, 93

pacing 143
painkillers 92, 93, 122, 284
parole 71
applications for 48, 53,
65, 145
breaches 45, 116, 129
violations 48, 100

parole board 65, 142
parole officer (PO) 100,
104, 285
paroxetine 266
patience, need for 76,
87, 94
penis presentation 228
personal hygiene 191–2
personality disorder 66
phone accounts 150–1
phone money 151–2
physical contact 225–8
PIN 78, 151
placement jails 53–6
awaiting movement
to 48
cons 55
drugs 117
educational
courses 135, 136–7
group activities 136
mainstream or all
protection 33, 49
medical needs 88–9
pros 54
purposes 48, 49
recognition of ASD
diagnosis 52
residential accomm-
odation 54, 55
serving sentence in 48
transportation 60–1
violence 53, 54, 55
working out 211–12
plausible denials 26
police
assaulting of
officers 30
body searches 36–7
co-operation with,
avoiding admitting
to 27
dogging (providing
police with
information) 53
raids 22–3, 29
watch house staffed by
police officers 30–1
police informants 32
politics/prison
politics 205, 219, 258

post-jail activities 279,
283–90
counting one's
blessings 288
PTSD 284, 285
study 287
telling people about
incarceration 288–90
urine tests 286
volunteering 287
work 287
see also pre-jail
activities
post-traumatic stress
disorder (PTSD) 284, 285
pregabalin 115
pre-jail activities 279
avoiding prison
stimuli 282
contacting mental
health services in
advance 281–2
martial arts 282–3
shaving one's
head 283
talking to ex-
prisoners 280–1
working out 282
see also post-jail
activities
preparing for the
day 164–5
pre-release
behaviour 220
prison account 77, 152–3
prison number 77–8
prisoner movement see
movement of prisoners
prisons see jails
protected inmates
children, avoiding
topic of 188, 189
movement of
prisoners 32–3
offers of
protection 223–5
reasons for going into
protection 31–3
where protection not a
choice 33–4

see also mainstream
inmates
protocol, prison 41, 70,
74, 212
psychiatric expert,
seeing 87, 95–8
psychologists 75–6
psychosis 66
public address (PA)
system 148–9

quetiapine (Seroquel) 39,
96, 115, 121

racial division 184–6
radios, in cell 190
ramping (searching for
contraband) 71, 168–9,
170, 244
random searches 169–70
rape 31, 83
reading 140, 202, 273
reception call 79, 151
reception jails 51–3
awaiting movement to
a placement jail 48
drugs 51
educational
courses 133
group activities 133
medical needs 51–2, 88
pros and cons 52
purposes 49
two-tier policy 33, 49
visits 51, 117
recidivist offenders 116
recreational drugs see
drugs
remand jails 28
body searches 36
drugs 50, 116
educational courses
and group
activities 133–4
feeling at ease in 85–6
medical needs 88
pros and cons 50
purposes 48
random searches 169

recognition of ASD
diagnosis 52
two-tier policy 33, 49
unit and cell
allocation 148
remanding in custody 28
awaiting
sentencing 48
awaiting trial 47–8
repetitive positive
thinking 274–5
residential
accommodation (res) 54,
55, 168–9
riot squads 170–1
risk assessment score 167
robbery 13, 19–20, 83
armed 19, 29, 33, 85
routine 80
'run-of-the-mill units' 12,
18, 56, 244, 246, 263

sales to prisoner (STP)
purchases 155–6, 199, 271
sanctuaries, finding 261
schizophrenics 66
screws see correctional
officers (COs)
searches
body searches 36–7, 75
cavity searches 37, 116
ramping (searching
for contraband) 71,
168–9, 170, 244
random 169–70
'seasoned' prisoners 81,
146, 217
segregation 68, 185
see also racial division
self-harming 94–5, 99
sentencing
custodial and
non-custodial
sentences 27
life imprisonment 217,
232, 241
placement jails,
serving in 48
post-sentencing 145
pre-sentencing 144–5

remanding in custody
awaiting 48
suspended
sentences 27
Serenity Prayer 88, 126
Serepax 45
serotonin 266
'severity' chart 83
sexual crimes 31
sharing a cell 194–203
basic behavioural
expectations 196–7
masturbation 197–8
potential areas of
conflict 198–202
general
cleanliness 200–1
ideological
clashes 201–2
lights out 199
showering 200
television 199
practicalities 195–6
soothing
techniques 202–3
see also doubling-up
(sharing a cell with
another inmate)
shaving one's head 81, 283
Shawshank Redemption,
The (King) 220
show, putting people
on 228–9
showering 75, 166, 193, 200
shy bladder syndrome
(paruresis) 234, 286
see also urine tests
(UTs)
silence, right to 24, 26
singling-out (having cell
to oneself) 259–60
sleep 130, 199, 265–6
smoking 77, 172–3
smoking gun 26–7
SNUs see special needs
units (SNUs)
social activities 131–3
cards 131, 132, 218
games 131–2, 218
group exercise 132

see also group
activities; social
advice; social
interaction
social advice 181–93
cell radios 190
children, avoiding
topic of 188–9
clever inmate 184
enforced
socialising 182–3
first names 192–3
music 189–90
opinionated
inmate 183
personal hygiene 191–2
racial divides 184–6
showering 193
telephones 190–1
TVs and movies 187–8
see also social
activities; social
interaction
social interaction 204–29
buy-ups 206–7
coping
mechanisms 266
fighting 218–20
gambling 209
getting goods into a
cell 208–9
going home
etiquette 220–1
intimate contact and
body exposure 225–8
offers of
protection 223–5
prison politics 205,
219, 258
respecting the
unit 217–18
standover 'men' 207–8
table etiquette 212–14
topics to avoid 221–3
transportation 60
visits 214–16
watch house/holding
cells 41–2
working out 209–12

see also group
activities; social
activities; social
advice
social navigation 42
solitary confinement 53,
105, 119, 161–2, 209, 267,
276
solution-based therapy
(SBT) 273–4
soothing techniques 202–
3, 259
special interests
(SIs) 125–6, 130, 252,
260–1
special needs units
(SNUs)
applying for 206
attending from
placement jails 55
confrontation,
avoiding 242–3, 244,
246
inmates without
mental health
conditions 67
looking down at
inmates from 67
non-existent,
where 68
persons with ASD
going to 62, 63–4
reasons for
attending 64, 68
as 'soft' option 67, 215
violence, low-level 63
staff training 172
standard operating
procedure (SOP) 103
standover 'men' 207–8
stereos 189, 202
STP see sales to prisoner
(STP) purchases
'street' criminals 64
street drugs 115, 117
stress management 99
strike action 175
see also hunger strikes
strip searches 170
study 287

suicide, jail 113
  see also self-harming
sunlight 266
support person 24
suspended sentences 27

table etiquette 212–14
tattoos 81, 166–7
telephones 190–1
  phone accounts 150–1
  phone calls 37–8
  phone money 151–2
television 187–8, 199,
270–1, 273
tellers (inmates thought
untrustworthy) 237
testifying against
others 32
tidying up 217
time alone 138–46
  courses 139–40
  drawing 144, 261
  exercise 139
  helping people with
    legal activities 140–1
  legal (pre-
    sentencing) 144–5
  legal (post-
    sentencing) 145
  parole
    applications 145
  reading 140
  walking 143
  writing 143–4, 261
toilet etiquette 196
topics to avoid 221–3
  children 188–9
tossing see ramping
(searching for
contraband)
tough units see Bronx
(tough) units
transportation 18, 57–61
  coping with 59–61
  placement jails 60–1

potential issues
  with 58–9
prison bus 57–8
reasons to address 57
social interaction 60
why inmates are in
  transit 59
trial, awaiting 47–8
tricyclic
antidepressants 122
turtles (correction
officers dealing with
violent inmates) 70, 238,
268
  see also correctional
    officers (COs)
28-day sanctions 100–1

undercover operatives 60
unit and cell
allocation 148
unlocking (opening
of cells around 7.30
am) 103–5, 111, 164
urine tests (UTs) 52–3,
114, 286
  and COs 163–4, 233–4
  see also drugs; shy
    bladder syndrome
    (paruresis)

Valium see diazepam
(Valium)
violence
  avoiding 241
  low-level, in SNUs 63
  placement jails 53,
    54, 55
  see also fighting
visits 156–8
  booking 156
  contact 156–7
  legal 216
  non-contact 157, 158
  reception jails 51, 117

social interaction 214–
16
types 156–7
unexpected 158
volunteering 287

walking 143
washing 218
watch house/holding
cells 30–46, 85
  ASD, inmates
    with 34–5
  ASD-specific
    issues 40–1
  behavioural
    conduct 41
  body searches 36–7
  identifying
    particulars 37
  interacting 41–2
    with the
      officers 43–4
  life in 40
  location 30
  mainstream
    inmates 31, 32
  medical needs 38–40
  phone calls 37–8
  points of note 44
  processing 35–6
  protected
    inmates 31–4
  social interaction 41–2
  social navigation 42–3
  staffed by police
    officers 30–1
weapons, homemade 176
white-collar crime 35
work 158–9, 287
workers units 242
working out 132, 209–12,
282
writing 143–4, 261

yoga 265